THE OTHER SIDE
of broken

THE OTHER SIDE
of broken

AN EMPATH'S GUIDE
TO OVERCOMING DEPRESSION

By Alisabeth Shelman

Copyright 2018

Cosmic Publishing

Salt Lake City, UT, USA

Copyright © Alisabeth Shelman, 2018

All rights reserved. No part of this book may be reproduced in any form without permission in writing from the author. Reviewers may quote brief passages in reviews.

Published 2018

ISBN: 9781980594871

DISCLAIMER

No part of this publication may be reproduced or transmitted in any form or by any means, mechanical or electronic, including photocopying or recording, or by any information storage and retrieval system, or transmitted by email without permission in writing from the author.

Neither the author nor the publisher assumes any responsibility for errors, omissions, or contrary interpretations of the subject matter herein. Any perceived slight of any individual or organization is purely unintentional.

Brand and product names are trademarks or registered trademarks of their respective owners.

Cover Design: Teba Coulson

Editing: Nicole Maestas

Dedication

To my Guides,
both in Spirit and in the Akasha,
who shared with me the wisdom of the Records,
who helped me align to my path
so I can help others align to theirs.

Table of Contents

Introduction
Chapter One: What's Happening to Me?.................... 1
Chapter Two: The Akashic Records 31
Chapter Three: Union with Your Body 41
Chapter Four: Managing Your Sensitivities............. 55
Chapter Five: Understanding and Utilizing Your Empathic Gift 73
Chapter Six: Finding the Beauty in Trauma............ 105
Chapter Seven: Embracing Your Role as a Healer .. 137
Conclusion 161
Acknowledgements 165
About the Author 168

The Breaking Open of the Day

It is in the breaking open of the day,
The sun is able to shine its light,
And darkness fades.
Every night, darkness returns,
And every morning,
The day breaks itself open across the sky.

Perhaps the very first daybreak,
Took a great amount of courage by the sun.
There was not yet knowing,
That when the light came,
Darkness would fade.

And there was not yet knowing,
How the light would impact everything on
Earth.
This daily courage soon turned into knowing.
This knowing eradicated any possible memory,
Of a day without light.

As we find ourselves shrouded in darkness,
We must have the courage to break ourselves
open,

And release all our distortions,
So we may shine our light.

This daily courage and conquering of fears
Must become our only way of existence.
We must eradicate all memory of choosing anything but this,
So our light may be a constant.
We must anchor into the knowing that when darkness comes,
The light ALWAYS comes shortly after.

Your world, and the world around you, needs you to shine your light.
It needs you to exhume all the places within you,
That does not allow your light to break free.

Let's do it together.
Break open with me.

XO,
Alise

Introduction

It was once quite common for me to lock myself away from the world, unable to manage everything I was feeling and the energy swirling all around me. Sensory stimulation would overwhelm me and leave me unable to take in more. Many times, I would plant myself in the darkness of my bedroom closet, attempting to push away the emotions and suffering of those whose energy I picked up that day.

It was years before the term Empath entered my vocabulary. I can't seem to recall where I first stumbled upon it or when it clicked into place. Once I found it, all the advice seemed to follow and I hung on for dear life hoping for answers. Hoping to find my way out of the overwhelm and depression that plagued me.

I thought that being empathic was why I spent half of my life depressed. If I could learn to manage this, I'd finally find a reason why nothing else seemed to work.

I followed the advice found in every article. I tried "protecting myself" from others' energy, by placing myself in an imaginary bubble. I tried discerning if what I was feeling was even mine. When an earache, headache, or any ache would hit me out of nowhere, I was quick to ask those around me who it belonged to. I also tried discerning if what I was feeling was mine, to then send it back to sender with love, assuming it had even been sent to me in the first place.

Trying to protect myself and questioning, *"Is this mine? Who does this energy belong to?"* didn't transmute the energy or allow for an understanding of what was taking place. It was a short-term strategy for something that required a long-term solution. This advice simply meant that in that moment I could pretend to have regained control. Oh, how I longed for a sense of control! So much about being empathic feels wildly helpless.

Experiencing the world in this way goes as far back as I can remember. As a child, I was deeply connected to the energy of all things unseen. I found myself in constant communion with the energy swirling all around me.

Energies from the present day.
Energies of those who lived in my home before me.
Energies of those who lived in my home in parallel dimensions.
Energies from other realms.
I was in communication with all of it.

I spent a lot of time alone and in small spaces. Closets were my favorite place to play. The daytime darkness was a welcome break from the intensity of a world too full to take in. It was more peaceful being all by myself. I could tune into and discern what energies were coming from where, without the bombardment of sensory overwhelm and those who shared the physical world with me.

As I got older, the constant perception of energy became unbearable. My connection gave way to darkness and was replaced with chronic depression and anxiety. Panic attacks and suicidal ideations peppered my teen years and early adulthood. I didn't know there was another way of being.

As an adult, I found myself retreating, once again, to the closet. Closing those doors was my way of shutting out the world and all it entailed. If I could shut out the world, then maybe I could stop the staggering emotions and sensations moving through me and all around me. I craved to experience me. Just me. Without the addition of anything else. Do you feel that way?

It took years before I fully understood the meaning and the higher truth about what was happening to me. Initially, I resisted. I wanted to be let off the hook. I wanted my life to be easy. Eventually, I learned to manage my sensitivities and turn on and off being empathic, like flipping a switch. I learned how to create a life that fully supports who I am and how I best function in the world.

I'm happy to say that depression and overwhelm are no longer my experience. I have reached a place of great joy with my abilities. I now use these abilities to help others and to serve my clients. Because I can feel what they are feeling, I see them, hear them and love them on the deepest of levels. In turn, I see, hear and love myself on the deepest of levels as well. As I use this gift to help others heal, in turn, I continue to help myself heal.

I have learned that being empathic is not just about being highly sensitive and absorbing the world around you. This definition is devoid of light. Being an Empath is about having an ability to authentically connect with the world around you. Within this ability to connect with the world, lies a channel to deeply connect with yourself. Through this connection, deep healing can take place.

For just a moment, I ask you to allow the possibility that you have been given a divine gift. Allow the possibility that with this gift, you may transform your inner world and help to shift your consciousness and the consciousness of the masses.

By opening to the energy that is all around you, and using it to move within, you bring light and joy into your life. A light and a joy that will automatically flow to those around you.

1
What's Happening to Me?

"I feel certain I am going mad again."
-Virginia Woolf

You've got the feels.
All of them.
His. Hers. Mine. Theirs.
The world's.
In addition to your own.

They seem to show up everywhere and out of nowhere. It's hard to put your finger on.

Anxieties.
Frustration.
Overwhelm.
Heartache. Headache.
All the aches.

You find yourself asking, *"Where does it come from?" "Why do I feel so much of everything and everyone that's all around me?"*

It's a lot.

Feeling it can quickly become drowning in it.

Isolated.
Alone.
Not enough.
Broken.
Lost. Lost cause.

You find yourself staying at home for fear of being overwhelmed. You question your ability to function in this world. You find yourself pondering over and over, *"Why me?" "Why don't I have what it takes to function as a "normal" person in this world?" "Am I broken?" "What do I do?" "Where do I go?" "How can I fix this?"* The unanswered questions plague you.

Some days you don't want to get out of bed, go to work, or do anything that involves other people. One more person dumping their problems on you might just be the breaking point. It's not that you don't want to help, you do. In fact, you have a deep desire to. It feels like helping others is a big part of why you're here. But a desire to help others takes a back seat to keeping your head above water. The longing to help is quickly outweighed by the need to simply get through the day. Where can there be purpose when you're just trying to survive?

You may have been told you're an Empath. And you've been told that as an Empath, you take in the energy that swirls all around you. Like a sponge, you absorb it. You take it in and it becomes you. Wherever you go, whomever you meet, you are subconsciously absorbing the energetic landscape. An absorption that gets so heavy and dense, you feel lost in it.

The common words of wisdom given as a means of coping with being empathic are: protect yourself from others. Zip yourself up. Cut yourself off. Lock up your energy in a bubble. I imagine you've heard this before. From friends on Facebook to most articles written about being empathic, the advice to protect yourself will be found.

The idea of removing yourself from the energy- may provide a sense of safety and comfort in a chaotic world. This perspective, of what it means to be empathic, unfortunately, only works short term. These words of wisdom act like a band-aid to what feels like a gushing bullet wound.

When we dissect the word Empath and look at the root meaning, we receive: caused to be in feeling.

Caused. To be. In feeling.
Of course.

And it's a beautiful thing. But it doesn't feel that way. Not right now anyways. It feels overwhelming, out of control, and pointless. It appears to be a big part of why it can be hard to pull yourself out of depression. Perhaps it is the cause of the downward spiral into depression. The weight of your own traumas and challenges are amplified by the traumas and challenges of the world around you. So, you isolate. You avoid certain people or situations. How could anyone expect you to carry all that weight and flow through the world with ease?

Oh ease! What a lovely concept. How can there be ease when as an Empath so much is happening at once? So. Fucking. Much.

Two massive things are taking place for you. First, your senses are operating on over-drive. One or more of your five physical senses (touch, taste, smell, sight, hearing) are doing more work than the average person. Your Central Nervous System is literally over-processing information in the physical world.

Through this over-processing, your senses are reaching a greater depth of information and sensory stimulation, creating a high level of sensitivity.

Lights are extra bright.
Noises are extra loud.
Smells are extra strong.
Touch is extra intense.

Taste is more complex.

All this information coming in from the world around you may feel like an assault; an attack on the Central Nervous System that yells back, *"Retreat! Retreat!"*

Second, you are feeling the experiences of others as though they are your own.

Sometimes, it shows up in your physical body. You question if it's from a stranger at the grocery store, your best friend, or the collective world at large. A headache that catches you off guard. A pain in your side. A kink in your neck. Sensations without a known cause.

Sometimes, it shows up in your emotional body. Grief. Sadness. Heartache. Anxiety. Depression. Anger. None of which make any sense why.

Sometimes, it shows up in your mental body. A phrase you would never say or a statement you would never speak makes its way into your mind.

Pictures pop into your head. Scenarios play out that you would not typically construct on your own. You find your thoughts spiraling out of control. Your brain often feels like it's on fire as it's inundated with overthinking and overanalyzing everything.

Sometimes, you feel it in your spiritual body. It comes as a knowing about someone or something. A higher perspective or foreboding. A deeper understanding or a forewarning. It's a reaching out into worlds beyond this one, a communication with something more. You feel it as energy, around you, around others, around plants, animals or things. You sense that there is so much more happening than what is seen with the naked eye.

And sometimes, it shows up in all four. It can be hard to differentiate between your mental, emotional, physical, and spiritual bodies and all the sensations that are taking place.

I understand.

I feel it too.
I've felt it my entire life.
All of it,
And then some.

> ### *Journaling*
> Take a moment and share your story with me. Write it down or draw a picture. Tell me what takes place for you in the day-to-day as an Empath.

I want you to know you're not alone. You're not alone in what you are feeling and the experiences you are having. There are other people just like you. Just like me. And there are other ways of being. It may be hard to imagine, but you don't have to feel like this forever. The more you understand what is happening to you, the more opportunity you have to shift it.

I am here with you now, to guide you from this state of overwhelm and depression into a life of ease and joy.

BORN FROM THE STARS
"93 percent stardust, with souls made of flames, we are all just stars that have people names."
– Nikita Gill

Before your body was birthed upon this Earth, the elements you are comprised of were birthed in the heart of a star. As part of that star, it is within your physical DNA that you shone brightly across the galaxy.

Queen of your own solar system.
Priestess of your domain.
Goddess of the light.
Giving warmth and life to the planets that encircled you.

Upon death, your star exploded, dispersing itself across the galaxy. Stardust landed upon the Earth and became the building blocks of your body. The iron in your blood, the calcium in your bones, and the oxygen in your lungs were given to you by the stars.

This is the history of your body.

In an interview with National Geographic, Iris Schrijer, co-author of Living with the Stars, says, *"Everything we are and everything in the universe and on Earth originated from Stardust, and it continually floats through us even today. It directly connects us to the universe, rebuilding our bodies over and again, over our lifetimes."* Co-author Kerel Schrijer states, *"We have stuff in us as old as the universe."*

While your physical body was being birthed in the heart of a star, your soul was birthed among them. As a soul, you may have lived many lifetimes in another solar system before staking your claim on your stardust and being birthed into this physical Earthly realm. This history of your soul is found in the Akashic Records, an ethereal library which contains the history of all creation. You can feel it for yourself too. There are common signs that your soul came from the stars:

- Do you find yourself looking to the stars for answers?
- Does your heart call out for home? Homesick for a place that can't be found?
- Do you feel different from the world around you? As though you don't belong?
- Have you found yourself thinking you're not from here? That you're possi bly alien?

There's a reason you feel this way. It's leading you to the truth of your soul's birth.

I want to take you back to the beginning of time. Even before time. It is from this perspective we reach a higher level of understanding about where you are right now and what you are experiencing. Before time, we find the story of your soul, and the story of the creation of all souls.

In the beginning, one was everything and everything was one. One took the name of Divine Source. And Divine Source was who would give birth and become the Creator of all Beings. Source understood that the only way to truly experience itself was to not be one with itself. The only way to truly see and understand self was through polarity and contrast. Thus, one became two. And with two allowed the generating force of all creation, giving birth to all components within the universe, including our souls.

Science calls this the Big Bang Theory. Before the Big Bang, there was simply dense energy. After the Big Bang, the dense energy became Hydrogen and Helium, which ultimately gave birth to all other creation.

The Akashic Records tells us that this dense energy, which I will refer to as Divine Source, was comprised of compassion, creativity, love, power, truth, and wisdom.

In the way that our bodies took on the elements of the stars, our soul took on all divine aspects of Source. You received this same ability to become a powerful creator of all things, a powerful creator of your life, to use contrast to better understand yourself in your divinity. You were given this ability, along with being empathic, to share with others. As an aspect of Source, each of us is holding a piece of the puzzle. As we come together in our divinity, we have the full picture of the divine, coming together as a unified whole, a physical representation of oneness. As we honor our divine creative power, we align with our light.

You are Divine. As the Divine, you are here to reclaim your birthright as Queen of your own solar system; Priestess of your own domain. You are not here to be depressed. It is something you absolutely will move beyond. Depression is simply one possible expression as the powerful creator of your reality. It is part of the contrast, the polarity, that can help you better understand who you are as the light. An extension of the individuation from Source. It is here you best understand light and dark. You better understand lack and abundance. You learn the difference between alignment and misalignment. The light, the abundance, the alignment is ever present as you stand in the remembrance of your origin, as you stand in your divinity and your creative power.

The Akashic Records continue to tell us that as your soul was birthed into being, it originated on a planet, within another solar system, separate from the one we live in today. We did not all come from the same place. Nor did everyone first originate on another planet.

But you my dear, as an Empath, searching the stars for answers, longing for home, you know in your heart, that not just your body, but also your soul came from the stars. A star system your soul still longs for and searches the sky over for answers. And it is that star system that your soul calls home. Your home in which everyone around you, was quite like you. So much so that the way you experienced your planet was the way that everyone experienced the planet. What mattered to you, mattered to everyone. It all began quite harmonious and lovely.

Just imagine.

Imagine being part of a world where everyone has an unwavering connection to Source. It is not possible to consciously make choices out of alignment with your divinity. Everyone is fully aware of how his or her choices impact others and always act according to the highest good of all, creating a utopian atmosphere. Because everyone acts from their light, all you see is their light. You learn that those around you are incapable of choosing harm or hurting others. Lies, deceit, and destruction simply don't exist. The moment you see shadow, the shadow shifts, because it is simply the awareness or consciousness of the shadow that has it shifting into the light.

Imagine being a part of a planet full of change agents. Visionaries with missions so big they want to shift their entire galaxy into alignment with the light. Everyone is deeply motivated to eradicate negativity and works together to make it happen. There is little thought, certainly no argument. Everyone dives into action, doing his or her part to create the intended transformation.

Imagine being from a place where everyone seeks to improve themselves and the world around them. They strive to make things better and better and better. There is no stagnancy, no mediocrity. Intuition is highly regarded. Intellect is leveraged and utilized to uphold high vibrations. Within everyone is a deep desire to help those from other solar systems uphold these vibrations and act from a place of connection and intuition.

Imagine a society operating on unconditional love. Tolerance. Compassion. Unity. All your emotional needs are instantly met. Relationships are the highest level of importance and everyone holds space for everyone else. It's a giant lovefest!

It is in those lifetimes before Earth, you became quite accustomed to your soul's expression as understood on its home planet. You lived among others who saw your world and understood it in the same way that you did. These traits became imprinted upon your soul and naturally express themselves into your human expression. Akin to being from one country and moving to another much later in life, you are accustomed to a way of living, to which most around you are also accustomed. The star you are from gives you the culture of your soul.

Then you came to Earth, the melting pot of our galaxy. Where everyone from every solar system comes together, but not for the same reasons. Some came because their home was destroyed, either by environmental problems or through the destruction of other not so kind and loving soul cultures. Some came to dim the light, to snuff out the soul's evolution. Some came to bring back hope, to uplift the low vibrations of the planet. Some came simply to tend to the Earth, to learn from the Earth, and be at harmony with her. Some came because of the karma they created, needing to transmute it. Some came for the fun of it, to experience the third dimensional world. On Earth, everyone sees the world differently, is motivated differently, and has different agendas.

You, my dear, came to shine the light. You chose to bring back hope and to help heal the wounding of those that now reside on this planet. You came to experience the deeper contrast, and in that contrast, you may better understand how your gifts can serve others on this Earthly realm.

I know. I feel your resistance. It feels too easy, too good to be true, too out of reach, and only real in the land of fairy tales.

It's easy to forget why you are here and what your purpose is, when the world doesn't make much sense. The dissonance, due to the contrast between where you are from and where you are now, on Earth, can at times be paralyzing. It's hard to wrap your mind around other's ability to consciously do harm in the world. It's hard to wrap your mind around the despondency or lack of desire others have to make this world a better place. It's hard to wrap your mind around people's lack of vision and innate drive to transmute negativity.

It's hard for your mind and almost impossible for your soul. It can be easy to get caught up in all the ways that life is hard and feels impossible. It can be easy to get stuck in what isn't working. But you must remember your vision. You must reach back to your original determination, your original decision to come to THIS planet. You are filled with a desire to serve. You are filled with a desire to live a life of purpose. You are filled with a desire to help others heal. And it is through this desire that you may find yourself in a state of hope, a state of action, and a state of unwavering question that you are here for a reason.

A big reason. A reason that your soul desperately wants you to remember.

YOUR ENERGY MATRIX

"In the moment you stop trying to conquer the labyrinth and simply inhabit it, you'll realize it was designed to hold safe as you explore what feels dangerous. You'll see that you're exactly where you're meant to be, meandering along a crooked path that is meant to lead you not onward, but inward."
-Martha Beck

As your physical body and your soul hold the DNA and history of the stars, your energy body expresses this truth. Have you heard of chakras, auras, and energy work? They are becoming more and more commonly known. What is less commonly known is the energy body in its entirety, your energy matrix. This is this energy body that reflects your star status.

As an embryo growing inside your Mother, everything you needed was provided for you. An umbilical cord fed you all the nutrients you needed to grow and develop. You were enveloped in a warm body of water, contained within a sack, gently held within the womb. Whatever micro and macro nutrients were required at any given moment during your development, your Mother's body found a way to create a perfect match for your needs.

As you are born from the womb of your Mother, you are held within the womb of the cosmos. Just as you are safe, protected, nurtured, and given everything you need as an embryo, the same is energetically true today.

You have an energetic umbilical cord that feeds you all you need to grow and develop. This is called your Godspark. It is connected to your thymic chakra, between your heart and throat chakras. It is through this Godspark that Source (your Cosmic Mother, the Creator of all Beings) feeds you vital life force energy. This vital life force energy pumps through your heart and courses through your veins, giving life to your being. Vital life force energy is what gives life to all beings. Also known as chi, it is the force that runs through and animates all.

The energy that pours into your Godspark is a perfect match for what you need in each moment. It reflects the energy of your Highest Self, the part of you that knows yourself as a divine being birthed from Source. It is the energy that feeds your soul and fills you with all you need to thrive on this Earthly realm. Through the Godspark, you remain energetically nurtured and fed on this planet.

As this Godspark feeds you vital life force energy, it moves from your thymic chakra to your heart. Your heart pumps this energy throughout your body. Moving down your torso, around your thighs, your legs. Moving all the way down to the tips of your toes. This energy moves across your shoulders, down your arms, to the tips of your fingers. It moves up around your neck and up to the crown of your head. Your body is immersed in golden light. It feeds your organs, muscles, tissues, bones, and all the spaces in between. As your body fills up, this energy expands and pours out all around you, enveloping you in a Golden Web. This web is akin to the sac of warm water that held you in your Mother's womb.

It is the Golden Web that keeps you in energetic integrity. It is an energetic boundary between you and the world. Your energy is your energy, and the energy that swirls all around you does not become you or plague you. The Golden Web is your natural cocoon of safety.

This energy continues to expand and pour all around you. Effusively. Like the layers of tissue and muscle that ensure your safety in the womb, this energy envelops you in perfect spheres. Sphere after sphere, cradling you in Source love and light. These spheres are layers and layers of your own vital life force energy surrounding you, radiating out all around you like a brilliant golden light.

As six spheres of love and light build up all around you, a final sphere of violet fire completes you, causing you to radiate like the sun, gifting you the ability to burn up anything in your atmosphere that is not in service of you. This violet fire ensures that whatever comes into your spheres is a vibrational match to you. Anything you experience must pass through this violet fire, through your spheres, and through your Golden Web to reach you. It is coming into your space for you. Nothing can survive moving into the heat of the sun, unless it is the same temperature of the sun, it must be a perfect match. What comes through your spheres and shows up in your web reflects you. It is a perfect match to you, showing up for you.

Exercise
FEEL YOUR GODSPARK AND GOLDEN WEB

Your Godspark comes straight up and out from your chest. Imagine a warm, brilliant white light coming out of your sternum. Like an umbilical cord, it is round and hollow, flowing vital life force energy. It can be anywhere from a few inches to 24 inches circumference.

Place your hands a few inches above and to the sides your sternum. Relax your fingers. Have the palms of your hands face each other. Slowly and gently move your hands in toward the sternum and slightly out and away from your sternum, as though your hands are gently, softly, pulsing in and out. Do this pulsation while moving your hands farther and farther away from each other. It is very subtle edge that you are feeling for. It is most easily felt when your hands are pulsing in versus pulsing out and away from one another. It may take a few tries.

If you are having difficulty finding it, you may want to start with your hands a few feet apart and slowly move them in toward one another, pulsing your hands while they move closer together. You may find that your hands don't want to move in any further. This is the edge of your Godspark. Your palms may feel warm and tingly once you find it.

Once you find the edge, you can move your hands out and away from your body to follow the direction of the spark. Sometimes it will move directly in front of you, sometimes it moves up and away from you, and in some cases, it moves down toward the ground.

To feel your Golden Web, stretch your arms all the way out to your side, hands facing out. Visualize it enveloping you. A few feet in front of, to the side of, behind, above and below you. Slightly bend your elbows. Your Golden Web lies right there on the edge, before your arms are fully extended. Slowly pulse your arms in and out, gently feeling for a subtle membrane. You may find your hands want to stay on the edge once you find the web. Again, you may feel your palms become warm and tingly as you find the edge.

Now, visualize golden light continuing to expand all around you, beyond your Golden Web. See it forming layers and layers of light. Tune into how far beyond your physical form your energy field stretches. Can you visualize it filling the room?

Does it expand through the floor and the ceiling?
Do you see it extending beyond your room?

Now visually take a step back and become your own observer. From a distance, see yourself receiving vital life force energy through your Godspark. See this energy pumping throughout your body, pouring out of you and forming the Golden Web that softly holds you. See the spheres of love and light expanding beyond the web. See yourself as a bright golden light. See how brilliantly and expansively you shine.

This.
This is your natural, divine state.
This is your truth.
You came to Earth with this brilliance.
This is the energetic framework you were designed with.

Each one of us has this energetic framework. This framework holds within it a natural form of energetic protection. It is this framework that shows us you have no need to protect yourself from others. You shine like a star and energetically operate like a star. Your light stretches far beyond your physical body. By shining your light, you bring warmth to the darkness.

As you open to this framework, you open to higher truth. The higher truth about being empathic. The truth that what you are feeling from all around you is showing you what is within you. It cannot come to you without being a perfect match to you. The energy you "pick up" from the world is showing up for you to show you what is within you. The heaviness around you is showing you the heaviness within you that is calling to be healed.

Everything that is "causing you to be in feeling" is causing you to feel yourself. This process becomes an accelerated tool for healing. It is the tool that accelerates your arrival at the destination of joy, flow, and total acceptance of self.

You see, being empathic is a call to be healed. It is a call to be healed so you may brightly shine your light and help others do the same.

The energies you are picking up from the world around you are a vibrational match to what is already within you. It is showing you, you. It is showing you the wounding within you that isn't allowing for the fullness of your light to shine through. Specifically, it is leading you back to the unhealed trauma of your past. Trauma from this lifetime and from past lifetimes.

Your empathic gift is asking you to break open the walls around your old wounds so you may shine your light and share it with the world.

2
The Akashic Records

"Sleep doesn't help if it's your soul that is tired."
-Sahil Vij

The Akashic Records contain every decision your soul has ever made. Often pictured as an ethereal library or great hall of records, I like to think of them as a Google search engine for your soul. In the records, you can ask anything that pertains to your soul's history. You may also begin to track your future. Your Akashic Records hold everything that has happened in this lifetime and all of your past lives, including the lifetimes before your incarnation on Earth. They continue all the way back to your individuation from Source, your original birth story.

It is here, from the stories of your past, we learn how to best move forward. We learn to fully heal past traumas and how to live a life of purpose. It is also here we may be in direct communication with your soul. And your soul has a lot to say about its current experience on Earth.

Waves crashing all around. Lost at sea. Swallowing water. Struggling to stay afloat.

Lying flat on the ground. Face down in the sand. A small pocket in the sand allowing for a shallow breath.

Hunched over in a hellacious storm. Wind whipping. Unable to move more than an inch at a time.

Hiding ten feet below the surface. Refusing to be seen or participate in the world.

Hanging out in outer space where you can't be touched. Massive distance between your and the Earthly noise.

These are all too common scenes in the records of an Empath. How you're feeling at soul level reflects how you are feeling about life on Earth. This is the first thing I check on when I enter a client's Akashic Records. I ask and images flood in. These scenes give us the first layer of insight into what your soul needs to thrive in this lifetime and on this planet.

However, you don't need direct access to the Akashic Records to begin cultivating a relationship with your soul. Your soul has a way of reaching out into the world to communicate with you what is held within your Akashic Records. Specifically, your soul is using your empathic gift as a main channel of communication. It is using this channel to connect you to the healing that is needed so you may step fully into your purpose. It is connecting you to suppressed emotions, walled off pains, and hidden traumas. All that you have tried to push out of sight and out of mind is asking, again and again, by your soul, to be seen.

It is only once you are willing to be fully with this communication that it will stop pestering you. Just like when someone is feeling ignored or misunderstood, they start talking louder and louder until someone finally listens. Your soul will do whatever it can to communicate to you what is and isn't working and what to do about it.

The communication may, at times, appear to be as emotionally developed as toddlers. It will quickly shift from tugging on your clothes to a full-blown tantrum on the living room floor to be seen and heard. The tantrums only stop when you start listening to the first gentle tug.

The stress, overwhelm, and depression you experience will only go away when you start listening to your gift. Depression is just another form of communication to help you do this.

DEPRESSION AS COMMUNICATION FROM THE SOUL

"I've been a seeker and still am, but I stopped asking the books and the stars. I started listening to the teaching of my soul."
-Rumi

In the summer of 2017, I did an Akashic Record study using a sample of 50 people with self-diagnosed and clinically diagnosed chronic depression. The intention of the study was to find the underlying root cause of lasting depression. I searched their Records to find what was happening at soul level that was creating the physical expression of depression.

There were few similarities in the physical world. There were a range of ages, genders, races, and socioeconomic backgrounds. I read the stories of their souls, discovering further diversity with a range of different past and present life traumas and different intensities of trauma. Some with trauma only from past-lives. Some with the majority of trauma from this lifetime. The specific energetic wounding left behind was different for every single person.

What they did all have in common was disconnection from their bodies, disconnection from Divine Source, and disconnection from their divine gifts. Because they had disconnected from their bodies as a result of trauma, the trauma was preventing them from receiving vital life force energy from Source at the fullest capacity. The trauma acted like filters, depressing the ability to receive through the Godspark, disallowing the spirit body full access to vital life force energy.

Let's look at what the word depression means:
De-press-ion
Noun
1. Feelings of severe despondency and dejection.
2. A long and severe recession in an economy or market.
3. The action of lowering something or pressing something down.

When we take the definitions in reverse what we get is the pressing down of the ability to receive vital life force energy. A long and severe length of time that this takes place results in feelings of severe despondency and dejection, thus resulting in depression.

From this study, we can see that the root cause of depression is lack of connection to Self, caused by a lack of connection to Divine Source.
Depression shows up when we have lost our ability to properly receive information through our

empathic gift. When the channel gets clogged, when we are inundated with overstimulation and when overwhelmed by feeling what everyone else is feeling, without having a known way to communicate with this energy, we separate from ourselves to cope. When trauma occurs, and there are not known coping skills, we also separate from ourselves to cope.

It is through this separation that we disconnect from our bodies. When we disconnect from our bodies, we disconnect from the communication of our soul, and we disconnect from the vital life force energy that Source is feeding us. We no longer feel the Godspark and the Golden Web, and we lose the natural spheres of love and light that surround us.

This causes a downward spiral. The longer we stay disconnected from our body, the longer our trauma and wounding can run the show and keeps us unwilling to reconnect with our body. Which spirals us downward again, as the universe must turn up the volume of stimulation and empathic overwhelm to get our attention in hopes that we reconnect with ourselves.

Depression then becomes an incredibly useful tool. Getting out of bed and making it through the day becomes the day's greatest success. We become incapable of moving forward. Depression becomes a messenger from our soul to say that what we are doing is NOT working. The way in which we are operating and trying to cope with our experiences is not bringing us the transmutation that is needed to clear out the energy and connect with the higher communication.

We are literally stopped in our tracks. Barely functioning. Giving us the space to look back. It is here that the only way forward is to take a clear look backward at the decisions that have been made, the choices that have brought you here, so you can make a new choice. A choice that is more aligned with the cravings of your soul to be a healer in this world, and to be able to make a difference.

We get to look back at how we have chosen to cope within the world. We get to look back at how we have chosen to manage what we don't understand. We get to look back at our trauma and give it space to communicate.

Depression is holding us accountable to our natural ability to communicate with the world around us and use that communication to bring us back to ourselves. It is holding sacred space for us to do deep inner work by coming back to our bodies, back to our connection with Source, and anchored back in our gifts.

Your soul is using your empathic ability to communicate with you what is needed to heal at soul level, what is needed to clear and complete your karma, and what is needed for you to fulfill your dharma; your life purpose.

REALIGNING WITH YOUR SOUL

You know now that you are a divine being from another planet who has come to Earth to share your healing gifts. Being an Empath is your primary gift. The depression you experience is a result of the disconnect from this truth, a disconnect from Source that has been amplified by the contrast of where you're from at soul level and your current experience on Earth. There are five key steps to take to overcome depression, to reclaim your life, and embrace your purpose as a healer:

STEP 1: Be in union with your body.
STEP 2: Manage your sensitivities.
STEP 3: Use being an Empath as a healing tool.
STEP 4: Find the beauty in trauma.
STEP 5: Step into your role as a Healer.

3
Union with Your Body

"Being human is not a limitation.
The human soul is bigger than the gods,
And the human mind is as immortal as the gods"
    -Don Miguel Ruiz

Step One in overcoming depression as an Empath is to connect with your body and embrace your physical form.

Have you heard the phrase being in your body? Think about it for a second. In. Your. Body.

Do images of taking a beautiful light being and shoving it into a small, dark, windowless, chamber come to mind? Does being in your body sound a bit suffocating to you? This feeling can be quite common for Empaths. The idea of being in your body may be overwhelming. It 100% felt that way for Elicia.

I met Elicia on Facebook. She reached out to me because she'd been working on her chakras for a long time, but her heart felt cold and closed. She wasn't sure why, but it was impacting her business and finances. She couldn't open fully to herself, therefore she didn't know how to open and serve those around her. Being human felt uncomfortable and foreign. She wanted to spend her days in the ethers, in outer space, where it was open and expansive. She also wanted to feel better about being on Earth.

Upon opening her Akashic Records, I fell head over heels in love with her soul. This isn't uncommon. Once I see all of someone, I can't help but love them. For Elicia, her energy was gloriously effusive and seeped out of every pore. A big, bright shining light, driven to be a guiding force. It felt amazing to be bathed in it. At first glance, it didn't make sense that her energy wasn't magnetizing the whole world. It certainly pulled me in. This dichotomy had her torn in two and only added to her frustration and overwhelm. I asked my Akashic Record Guides where the disconnect was. They took me all the way back to the beginning of time and showed me that her

Soul was replaying the memory of her individuation from Source, when she was birthed from the Divine and into the cosmos. The freedom and expansion of this birth was full of orgasmic creative power. She experienced herself as a part of everything, yet with unlimited possibilities of how she could express herself in contrast to the worlds around her. This fondly held memory sharply contrasted to her memory of being born on Earth. Her first breath on Earth, where she was pulled into her physical being, was unexpected and traumatic. It was nothing like her original birth. Confined in her body, she felt limited and powerless.

At a subconscious level, she repeated over and over, *"I don't fit in this body. I don't belong here. I don't want to be here. I didn't choose this."* This mental loop consumed her and closed her heart. And she left. She left her body behind and floated in the ethers. Spending most her time in outer space, where she felt comfortable among the stars, where she knew how to shine her light and be big and bright. But no one here on Earth could see that light, until she was willing to bring it into her body.

I've had several clients who believed their body could not possibly contain the immense amount of energy their soul is comprised of. The idea of being in their body felt limiting, exhausting and overwhelming. The human form was perceived as *"too damn dense"*. They felt expected to continue to shine bright enough that the world around them could still see them despite the density. *"It's too much!"* they would tell me. Any present-life physical trauma only added to the density.

Though I may use the term, being in your body, and it's a term I hear in the spiritual community often, it's not about being weighed down by your body. I'd like to think of it instead as being one with your body. Getting *"in your body"* is about calling yourself back to yourself. It is a union.

You are: In. Union. With. Your. Body.

This union is about being fully present, grounded, right here, right now, living your life. It's about being awake and conscious, available to make new decisions and creatively express yourself however you see fit. You see, when you are not in your body, it's like holding up a vacancy sign. Something else can come in and take over your life.

That something else is typically societal conditioning. It's the inherited beliefs from your parents and grandparents. It's the programming from past lives. It's the choices you made 20 years ago, that don't make sense for you today, but you aren't here to do anything about changing it.

You're somewhere else.

You may just be hanging out right next to your body, close enough to watch over it. Or you may be all the way in outer space. Surfing the ethers, spending time where you may feel more comfortable, away from all the thoughts, the emotions and the required actions of your day-to-day life.

Have you ever driven somewhere and once you arrive, you don't remember the drive? You're not entirely sure how you even got there? But it's the same path you take every time and you managed to get there by muscle memory.

This is what it's like living life outside of union with your body. The muscle memory of your conditioning and programming will get you where you're going, but you aren't along for the ride. You miss the beautiful sunset along the way. Or you miss the cute guy that was in the car next to you. These may be minor, unimportant things, until they're not. Until the sunset that you didn't see becomes the deer that slams into the front of your car and shakes you back to reality. Until that cute boy driving next to you becomes the road closure that wasn't there the day before and you don't notice until it's too late.

Our muscle memory can only take us so far. As the world around us changes, we need to keep up. When you outgrow an old way of being and an old way of seeing the world, if you aren't present for it, destruction, pain or suffering may take its place.

By consciously choosing to be in union your body, you are placing yourself back in the driver seat. It is here that you are most able to process the information that is communicating to you through the energy you are empathically connecting with. It is here that you are most able to connect with your intuition. It is here that you are most capable of experiencing joy and getting on the other side of depression.

When your spirit body is in union with your physical body, you are most energetically expansive. You can flow your creative energy out into the world, actively creating your desires. When you are outside of union with your body, your body runs on autopilot, using subconscious programming and conditioning to make choices for you.

Having subconscious programming and conditioning making choices for you means that your wounding from old traumas is being projected out into the world, determining the vibration of what you receive in life and what you are seeing as your reality. The wounds become in charge of what happens, rather than you being in charge of what happens.

Yes, there are parts of this life that are heavy and dense. Your thoughts may seem to control you, your emotions may feel like they are pulling you under, but this is only because you aren't present. Your consciousness is required to observe those thoughts and to properly honor those emotions.

It's time to be in union with your body. This is where your body and your soul work in co-creation, together, as partners, helping each other grow and expand beyond the capability of what one could do on its own.

It is in this place of union that you were designed to best function on Earth. It is in this space you most actively discover the inherent wisdom within you and all around you. The more you are in union with yourself, the more creative power you have to move your purpose into the world, the more creative power you have to build the life you desire. It is in this union that you can choose joy.

With this shift in perspective, Elicia cultivated a love of the physical world. She no longer felt confined when trying to "shove herself into her body." She found the expansion of this union with her physical form. She began to see the beauty of her humanity. The more she found the joy in the physical, the more her heart opened. The brighter her light shined. That effusive energy I found hidden in the records is now palpable on this Earthly realm.

Of all the Empaths I've worked with over the years, there hasn't been one who hasn't spent major chunks of their life outside their body as a result of trauma or "not wanting to be here."

Trauma is often the reason we leave our body in the first place. When the world does not feel safe, when we have not yet learned the tools to manage our emotions, nor the tools to understand our empathic nature, leaving the body becomes a coping mechanism. It is a way to avoid the pain and suffering present in this world.

And it works. Really well. Short term.

When it becomes a long-term mechanism for what should be a short-term response, this is where our car starts to crash, creating a vicious downward cycle. The car crashes, resulting in more trauma, resulting in more desire to leave the body, resulting in more car crashes. Trauma gets piled on top of trauma, on top of trauma. The ability to feel safe in your body seems farther and farther away.

The key to breaking the cycle is to get back in union with your body, get back into the driver seat, back into conscious choice so you can start moving in a new direction. Breath will guide you there and keep you anchored, so you can consciously make the choices that will help you thrive.

> *"We don't receive wisdom, we must discover it for ourselves after a journey that no one can take for us or spare us."*
> -Marcel Proust

Exercise

Take a moment. Take a breath. Tune in. See if you can find where you energetically show up in relationship to your body. Ask, *"Where am I in relationship to my body?"* and pause.

Are you a few feet in front of your body? Just to the side? All the way in outer space? All of the above? You may find your energy is scattered into a million pieces, trying to control all the different aspects of your life outside of your body, outside of your true place of power.

As you find your energy body, call yourself back to yourself. Invite your energy body to connect with your physical form while taking three deep breaths. Slow down your breath, bring your inhale all the way down to your diaphragm, expand your belly, your lungs and all the way up to your third eye. Then, slowly exhale back down into your diaphragm. Allowing yourself three of these deep breaths, coupled with some big sighs, or possibly groans, on the exhale will bring you back to center and fully rooted into full awareness.

Say out loud: *"I am calling myself back to myself."* Take another deep breath. Try it again: *"I am calling myself back to myself."* One more breath. One more invitation: *"I am calling myself back to myself."*

Visualize all the pieces of you flowing back into union with your body. See the pieces connecting, coming together and reaching a place of partnership with your physical form. Sigh out. You may feel an anchoring in as you settle into this union. A weighted presence that says, *"I'm here."*

Feels good, doesn't it?

95% of people I've worked with find union with their body through a few deep breaths and a request to be in union with their body. Having this be a part of your daily practice will help you to become more and more comfortable with being in your body and will show your energy body that it is now safe to be here. The presence you can hold for yourself daily with this practice, will bring healing to the wounded parts of yourself that do not feel safe. It will show your wounds that it's okay now. No longer do you have to hide. No longer do you need to remain in fight or flight.

Coming into union, you will hear your Higher Self say, *"I am here now. To hold you. We will do this together."*

4
Managing Your Sensitivities

"Sometimes it takes darkness and the sweet confinement of your aloneness to learn anything and anyone that does not bring you alive is too small for you"
-David Whyte

Step Two is about being able to discern the difference between being highly sensitive and being empathic, so you may manage your sensitivities. You need to know which gift is creating your experience, so you know what tools to utilize.

According to Dr. Elaine Aron from the Foundation for the Study of Highly Sensitive Persons (HSP's), 15-20% of the Earth's population is highly sensitive. There is no documented consensus on how much of the population is empathic. The most common range I've seen is 3-5%. This shows us that not every Highly Sensitive Person is empathic, but we do know every Empath is also a Highly Sensitive Person.

Remember, two very different processes are taking place and should not be confused with one another. The better you understand what is taking place, the greater your ability to shift from a state of overwhelm and anxiety to a state of ease and joy.

Do you recall that one of the main things happening to you as an Empath is that your Central Nervous System is operating on overdrive? This is what creates your sensitivities. You are over processing sensory information. This over processing of information means that you can reach a greater depth of information in the world around you. This depth can create an intensity or harshness in the way you receive the world.

You see more.
You hear more.
You smell more.
You taste more.
You feel more.

You may feel the anger radiating off a lover during a fight. You may feel the pulse of social anxiety flowing from an introvert at a party. Or the joy of a child as she laughs and plays.

You aren't absorbing these emotions. Your sensitivities are increasing the potency of your awareness.

When unmanaged, the potency can be unbearable. It is in honoring your sensitivities that they begin to work for you rather than against you. There is a fine line, a breaking point for each of us, where sensitivity turns to overwhelm, stressed out and run-down. There are four keys to ensuring you don't hit that breaking point:

1. Know your limits.
2. Be prepared.
3. Schedule regular self-care and alone time.
4. Know how to decompress once the line .
   has been crossed.

Key #1- Know Your Limits

Crossing your limits translates into physical discomfort. Headaches and fatigue are the most common responses to overstimulation. As you bring awareness to the beginning stages of the sudden onset of fatigue and headaches, you bring awareness to your sensory boundaries. Crossing the limit also often results in leaving your body to not have to deal with the stress and overwhelm. It can throw you back into the vicious cycle of letting your wounding run your life.

As you move through your day and spend time in different environments, pay attention to what feels like "too much." Is there a smell that's too strong? A certain amount of people in a room that crosses you into the threshold of overwhelm? Are there particular lights that seem to give you a headache?

I have learned that indoor malls are a very difficult place for me. I am certain never to walk past any stores that heavily perfume their space. Candle stores are a definite no-go. Malls are taxing for almost every Highly Sensitive Person I've talked to. All the smells, the people, the harsh lights, the chemicals in the fabrics of the clothing, it adds up quickly. I have about a 20 to 30-minute time span I can spend before I start to unravel. Once the unraveling begins it can take quite some time to recover. Twenty minutes of overstimulation may mean anywhere from two hours of recovery to two days. It is never worth crossing the line, except to reaffirm where your boundaries are and that you are willing to commit to them. Hey, there's something for you in every experience, right?

Key #2 - Be Prepared

The better I understand my limits, the better I can prepare myself and prevent overstimulation. I choose outdoor malls over indoor malls. Same goes for concerts. Outdoor venues seem to help reduce the overstimulation. I know when touch can feed me or drain me and I eat as cleanly as possible as not to inundate my taste buds (and body) with pesticides.

Traveling exhausts me. Especially flying. If I'll be spending a day traveling, I know I'll need the next day off from doing anything, especially working with clients. I know I'll need an "emergency" salt bath and that I'll most likely sleep 10-12 hours that night. It's simply what my body needs and ensures that I'm back to homeostasis as quickly as possible. Planning may also include planning the recovery if it's not in the cards to avoid overstimulation.

Outside of long days of travel, it's incredibly rare for me to get overstimulated. I have a sensory kit that I take with me wherever I go. It includes earplugs, sunglasses, a handkerchief, ear buds for music, an eye mask and a water bottle. I'll use earplugs in any noisy environment. Sunglasses may be used inside if lights are too bright. The handkerchief is to cover my nose when smells are too strong. The eye mask I might use on the ride home from a rowdy event to help relax my Central Nervous System. And water is a mandatory item to keep nearby always.

The key here is to manage your senses through preparation. Know what you are getting yourself into as you plan outings and prepare accordingly. Make sure a recovery phase is built into your schedule as needed.

> *Journaling*
>
> Take a moment and journal about where your boundaries currently lie. Do you have a sense of your own limits? What are some environments that tend to exhaust you?

> *Purse Preparedness Kit*
> Items to keep with you always to help prevent overstimulation or to help recover from it:
> - Sunglasses
> - Ear plugs
> - Eye mask
> - Bottle of water
> - Handkerchief
> - Headphones

Key #3- Regular Self-care

Regular self-care and alone time ensures you are filled up, so when you venture out into the world you have more capacity to be there.

What does self-care look like for you? For me, it's actively indulging my senses in a way that brings joy and pleasure. Actively indulging my senses means that I am in control of my environment and filling it with things I love.

For example, my absolute favorite thing is to eat Honey Mama's Raw Rose and Lavender

Chocolate, while taking an Epsom salt bath and listening to Oh Wonder in the candlelight. I'll close my eyes while sinking my teeth into the chocolate, bathing my taste buds in bliss. Then, I'll focus on just the music, letting it wash over my body while singing along. Then, I'll watch the candlelight dance across the wall. I focus on just one thing at a time, each thing being something I adore and fully want to receive into my space.

Another way I indulge my senses happens while hiking. I like to go by myself and walk along the stream that runs a few miles from my home. As I walk by the trees, I touch their leaves. I contrast the smoothness of the leaves against the texture of the bark. I place my hands in the stream and let it run over me. I stand open and hungry in the sun, drinking up the vitamin D.

By actively immersing myself in my senses, the world around me stops being external, chaotic noise and becomes a part of my being, another way of finding joyful union.

Most of the time, self-care means being alone. Fully alone. Alone time doesn't mean watching TV or eating mindlessly. Alone time means fully being with yourself, devoid of unnecessary stimuli. Alone time means that you are void of external energetic influence. You are completely with yourself. This allows you to decompress from stimulation overload. It gives you space to really get to know yourself and what it feels like to only be in your energy. It is here where I remove the sensory stimuli and enjoy being in the stillness, the silence, the pause between movement. It is in the pause, spending time with yourself, where you get to know yourself individuated from the energy of others. This allows you to know when your experience is due to having a deep awareness of the world around you or that you're receiving communication that is for you. This is an important foundational skill to have when utilizing your empathic gift.

Think of something small you can do today to bring in self-care. Maybe it's a 5-minute pause from this book, where you simply close your eyes and be with your breath. Immerse yourself in the ebb and flow as it moves in and out of your body, tuning into your natural rhythm. Maybe it's spending an extra 5 minutes in the shower, allowing the negative ions from the rushing water to lull you into relaxation, for just a moment, letting go of the to-do's and simply being with yourself.

Know that it's vital to keep your cup full. *"You cannot pour from an empty vessel."* Scheduling pockets of time for yourself throughout the day and big chunks throughout the week prevents your body from needing to slow you down with fatigue or even illness.

Journaling

What does self-care look like for you? Where are there gaps in your self-care? Where in your schedule is it most important to be getting more you time?

Key #4 - Know How to Decompress

It's common for people to describe being empathic as "one who absorbs the emotions of others." This has nothing to do with being empathic and everything to do with being a Highly Sensitive Person and not having the tools to properly process emotion and transmute energy. Sensitivity crosses the threshold between this is mine and this is yours. Think of it this way: imagine that as your senses are processing the world around you, it is as though they are reaching out into the world to gather the information and bring it back to your body. Being highly sensitive means that you are reaching further out into the world. You are crossing thresholds and barriers of the physical delineation of mine versus yours.

Crossing this threshold can take on the appearance of absorbing other people emotions. It is the sensitivity that tunes into the emotional frequency the other person is emitting. Absorption simply means that you picked up on the energy and don't have the skillset to process emotion or transmute energy.

You need to be sure you are moving the information all the way through your body. Absorption is taking place because you've stopped the processing. You may have stopped the processing because you felt overwhelmed by what was coming through or because it pushed you over the limit. Or you just don't know what to do with it.

Movement is a wonderful way to move the energy all the way through you. Dance is my favorite way to do this. I turn off the lights in my living room and move it through me.

Transmuting energy means that you are changing it from one form to another. We are shifting the density of stress and overwhelm to a lighter state of peace and relaxation. You don't have to dance it out. There are many ways to move it through you.

Shake out the energy.
Run until you cry.
Scream into a pillow.
Hit a speed bag.

Walk around your house groaning.

Groaning is my personal favorite on that list. These are all wonderful ways to complete the process and avoid "absorption." Once you've moved the energy through you, or as you are moving it through you, be sure to drink water.

Drinking water is a way to create a strong foundation for an HSP to not cross the line. Once the line has been crossed, drink more water to help your body manage the overstimulation. Remember that your system is over processing. It needs water to help lubricate this processing and not become too taxing on your body.

Another wonderful way to support your body in decompressing is with baking soda and Epsom salt baths.

Naps are also a great recovery tool. Twenty minutes of shutting out the world, turning off all external processing, allowing your body to use all its energy to bring balance and healing, it's a beautiful thing. Grab your softest blanket and cuddle up!

These energy transmutations do not have to be done in any particular order, nor do they all have o be done at once. Play around. Find what works best for you and allow inspiration to guide you.

Once you have managed your sensitivities, there is a lot more energetic space for you to be with what is showing up for you empathically. If you are overstimulated, your intuition will shut down to reduce the "noise." Following these four keys sets you up for the highest level of success to shift your empathic gift into the tool for accelerated healing it's designed to be!

Journaling

Where in life are you most needing to better manage your sensitivities? Where is the most important place for you to focus right now? Is there anyone you want or need to share this information with so they can be aware of your needs and help support you?

Formula For Water Intake

Your body weight _____ /2 =
_____ ounces to be drinking every day.

Add an extra 20 ounces for being a Highly Sensitive Person. This is the minimum amount of purified water to be drinking every day.

Salt Bath Energy Detox

2 cups baking soda

2 cups Epsom salt

16 oz hydrogen peroxide

4 drops lavender essential oil

The bath is a wonderful way to come back to yourself after the line has been crossed.

5
Understanding and Utilizing Your Empathic Gifts

"It's all connected. Your gifts, your circumstances, your purpose, Your imperfections, your journey, your destiny. It's molding you. Embrace it."
- Unknown

Part One
UNDERSTANDING YOUR
EMPATHIC GIFT

Step Three is understanding the higher truth about what's taking place for you as an Empath.

When we look to the world around us to define what it means to be an Empath, the most common definition found is "one who absorbs the emotions of others." Many articles then go on to explain that because Empaths absorb the emotions around them, there is a tendency to be a people-pleaser, to be ruled by the emotions of others and to be an over-giver.

The advice for management is centered around how it's important for you to protect yourself.

Because you are absorbing the world around you and it's causing you to feel and do all these things that don't serve you, you need to protect yourself from other people. You need to cut yourself of from being receptive to the world around you. Additional advice will tell you to question if what you are feeling is yours. If you can delineate your own emotions from others, you can release that which is not your own, or send it back to where it came from.

Conceptually, it may make sense. If I'm absorbing the world around me without choice, then yes, I must protect myself by placing myself in a bubble. Unfortunately, this does not have the desired impact.

The idea that you are willy-nilly absorbing the world around you is incredibly disempowering. This perspective takes you out of a place of choice and creates the perception that the world is happening to you and not for you.

The world is always happening for you.

It is a mirror.
A reflection of you.
It does not create you.
You create it.

Believing that the world around you is in charge of your experience is debilitating. It allows for victim mentality to take the stage and to anchor in a low vibration of helplessness and blame. Joy cannot be found here, just the comfort of remaining in the same low vibrational state. Feeling good because you are familiar with where you are is grossly removed from the vibration of joy. And it's a gross disconnect from yourself and the beauty of the world.

When you shield yourself from the world, cut yourself off, or zip yourself up, you create a story that you require protection from the world. Anything we require protection from is then seen as unsafe. When you see the world as unsafe, this story moves you into separation, moves you into judgment and moves you into fear. It is a recipe for a life of density and cycling in and out of depression.

You are not an emotional and energetic sponge. You are not feeling the way you do because you walked out of the door and into a mad world. Yes, the world is full of reasons to be mad, hurt, overwhelmed, stressed out, and broken. It's also full of reasons to be happy, healed, fulfilled, peaceful and whole. You feel the way you do, broken down, because you have not yet learned how to manage your physical being and intuitive gifts. You haven't learned how to honor your sensitivities and embrace the beauty in being empathic.

It's time to let go of the idea that you are an energetic sponge without choice about what is happening to you. I am here to hold space for your highest self and your deepest truth. I am here for you, the authentic you, the part of you that knows in your heart you are here for a bigger reason then walking through life in a bubble. I'm holding space for the part of you that wants to shout from the mountain tops, *"I'm a mother fuckin' alien and I'm here to change the world!"*

WHY IS THERE SO MUCH CONFUSION?

Having scoured dozens of articles on the internet about what it means to be an Empath, it became incredibly clear that most confuse being highly sensitive, intuitive, empathetic, and empathic with one another, as though they are all the same thing or all parts of one bigger whole. There is so much overlap, confusion often ensues, with little understanding of why it matters to know the difference.

In addition, every Empath is also a Highly Sensitive Person. However, not every Highly Sensitive Person is an Empath. Remember, 15-20% of the world's population is highly sensitive. Only 3-5% of the population is empathic, yet little to no distinction is made between the two.

It's especially hard to tell the difference for yourself when constantly being overstimulated. When sensitivities are not being managed, there can be so much energetic chaos, coupled with fatigue, that the ability to distinguish what is truly happening diminishes immensely. It is hard to trust your inner guidance with so much external noise.

You must first learn to manage your sensitivities before you can fully understand and work with your empathic gift. Without managing sensitivities, you will stay stuck in a disempowered state and in the depression cycle.

Let's get crystal clear on the differences.

Highly sensitive: Your physical senses are over-processing, giving you a greater depth of information in the physical world around you. *"I am exhausted from the bright lights and noise."*

Intuitive: Knowing beyond reason. Having information without "reasonable" explanation. *"I* *understand without having external reason to understand."*

Empathetic: An ability to understand and share the feelings of another. *"I understand because I have felt what you are feeling or I can imagine what you might be feeling given your circumstances."*

Empathic: Experiencing what others are experiencing as though you are generating or causing the experience. *"I feel you. Completely. I feel your heartache as though it is my own heartache. There is no delineation between you and me as energy beings."*

If you are identifying yourself as an Empath when you are not, you will be putting a lot of energy into something that doesn't even apply to you, therefore will not serve you. You will be adding to your fatigue and confusion. Without fully understanding where you are now, it doesn't matter where you want to go, it will be incredibly difficult to get there because you won't know which way to turn.

If you are a Highly Sensitive Person and not an Empath and suffer from depression, the depression you are experiencing and why you are experiencing it may be incredibly different than what is experienced by an Empath. Learning to manage your sensitivities will absolutely help, but will not give you the full picture. It's like using a compass that points East instead of North. It will not get you where you want to go. There are solutions out there for you that you will not find here.

Therefore, it's important to distinguish between the fine line of, *"Do I have an awareness of my friend having a headache because I'm finely attuned to sensing the world around me?"* OR *"Am I fully experiencing the headache as my own because I am empathically connecting to my friend?"*

THE HIGHER TRUTH OF BEING EMPATHIC

The true definition of being an Empath is having the ability to feel that of others; you feel their experiences as though they are your own.

As though.
They are.
Your own.
No delineation.
No threshold.

It is here we find the difference between being able to tune into what someone else is feeling versus experiencing what they are feeling as though you are the one feeling and generating the thought, emotion or physical state.

As a Highly Sensitive Person, you have a heightened awareness of the emotional state of those around you. You can sense emotions radiating off others, sometimes so potently, it can be unconsciously perceived as your own.

As an Empath, you are able to feel the emotion so intensely, it is as though the emotion is coming from you, as though you are the generator of the emotion, or experience.

By connecting to what is within others you are being shown what is within you. You are able to feel that of others to help you identify what is within you that wants to be seen and healed.

This is how being empathic becomes an accelerated tool for healing. What you are feeling is showing up for you, calling you forward, to heal the unhealed traumas that are ready to come to resolution, so you may glean the gifts they offer.

You feel that of others as though it is your own because it is a vibrational match to what is already inside you. It is an accelerated tool for healing by bringing to your awareness the trauma or suppressed emotion that wants to be healed and is asking for your attention. That which is ready to be healed is calling to you, you need not actively seek it out.

As an Empath, you are a natural born healer. You have an innate awareness to tune into that which wants to be healed, and an activated tool for identifying it. You are accelerating your own healing so that you may learn how to heal and help others do the same.

As you learn to work with your gift, you are able to hold space for others, and tune into their experiences so you may know how to best help them heal. This is one of the most intimate ways in which you can connect with another being. You have the gift to fully see, hear, and feel another exactly as they are.

When you are holding space for the healing of another, what you empathically tune into is showing up for their benefit in addition to your own. Ultimately, the message is always for you. Even as you help others, their lessons are your lessons. You will continue to attract the people and circumstances into your life to ensure your continued healing and ultimate mastery of helping others heals as well.

As you anchor into this new understanding of what it means to be an Empath, the question, *"How do I know if what I am feeling is my own?"* becomes irrelevant. There is no need to question who this energy belongs to because we now know the energy is showing up for you. You are feeling what you are feeling because it is a vibrational match to you, showing up as a tool for healing.

Despite any lists you may find out there or how many psychics may have told you it's true, the real self-assessment test is you. Does it feel true for you that you have been experiencing other's experiences as though they are your own? Either physically, mentally, emotionally, spiritually or all the above? You are your own best expert. You know better than anyone what is true for you.

As a true Empath, simply managing your sensitivities will not bring you to a place of joy. You have come here with a specific purpose that can't be fulfilled without the realization that you are a Healer. You, my dear friend, are deeply connected to the other side. It is only through this expression of your divine self that you will anchor into a state of joy and bliss in this physical realm.

You look to the stars because it's where you came from. You are looking to the stars to come back to your soul. And your soul is telling you this truth.

Part Two
UTLIZING YOUR EMPATHIC GIFT

"Your purpose in life is to use your gifts and talents to help other people. Your journey in life teaches you how to do that."
-Tom Krause

Using the intuition you already possess, you may begin to open yourself up to the guidance that is coming through your empathic gift. It will bring you clarity on how it can propel you forward rather than hold you back or take you under. Remember, being an Empath is a healing tool. What's coming through your empathic channel is showing up for.

Quite a few years back, I spent a day at a business retreat. At the time, I was advocating suicide prevention and shared such at the retreat. Afterwards, another attendee came up to me and shared with me that her friend had just passed by suicide the week prior. I hugged her and held her as she shared her experience with me.

When I got home that night I was completely overwhelmed. My chest and throat were tight. My heart hurt. My head was pounding. I was on the verge of having a panic attack. I quickly shut myself in my closet, away from the world, as was my coping mechanism at the time. As I sat in the dark, asking the universe to take this pain away from me, it is here that I started to unravel the truth about being empathic. I realized that this pain I was feeling was mine. Her pain simply showed me my pain that had yet to be processed.

I still hadn't worked through my brother's suicide which had been four years prior. In fact, I had kept the event so far from my mind, it was as though I never had a big brother at all. If I didn't have a big brother, I didn't have to mourn his loss or work through the guilt. So, I ignored it, for years. I tried to suppress it and it showed up in my life in other ways, such as meeting this woman, so that I could finally face it and start to work through it. By taking ownership of how this energy was for me, I was able to begin processing and working through my brother's death.

OPENING TO COMMUNICATION

Have you ever mulled something over in your head and can't seem to figure anything out, but the moment you put it out there, you ask someone on Facebook or schedule a session with your Coach, the answer comes to you? You didn't need the outside world to answer for you, you simply needed to get the question out of you, to see the question, so you could see the answer. This is the value of communicating with the energies that have presented themselves to you.

We can begin communicating using our intuition to talk to what is showing up. If anger is showing up, we will talk to the anger. If it's a headache, we'll talk to the headache. Whatever it is, intuitive inquiry will take us where we need to go.

Intuition flows like water and questions are like the river bank that contain and direct the flow. The higher the quality of questions, the stronger the riverbank to support the river.

Before starting to process the information, make sure you have built the foundation of managing your sensitivities and decompressing from those sensitivities.

We all have the ability to communicate with any and all things. Your sensitivities encourage this communication and allow for greater receptivity. Some energies may be easier than others, and they might all take practice to learn the language. But with enough time and effort, you could communicate with anything from the chair tucked under your desk to light beings from other realms.

When you boil it all down, everything is energy communicating with energy. You are made up of energy and space. So is the chair and so are the light beings from other realms. Just as I can fluently communicate with energy, so can you.

Be aware of the mindset that if you are intuitive it's because you were born that way and it's not something you can learn or develop. This simply isn't true. Cultivating your intuition is no different than learning a new language. Learning a new language take times, effort, intention and practice. The only difference is you aren't taking a class, you are learning by immersion.

Intuition is an incredibly receptive, feminine process. It is about energetically opening to receive the information. There isn't anything that really needs to be done, you simply allow.

Most Empaths receive their intuition through their sensitivities. Through your ability to access a greater depth of information from the world around you, you begin to connect to that which may be unknown or unseen by others. It is through this over processing that we reach the realm of intuition.

According to Merriam-Webster, intuition is defined as follows:
1. Quick and ready insight
2. a. Immediate apprehension or cognition.
   b. Knowledge or conviction gained by intuition.
   c. The power or faculty of attaining direct. knowledge or cognition without evident ra tional thought and inference.

The last one is my favorite in which I sum it up as: knowing something beyond reason.

For someone who is not highly sensitive, the range of information that is deemed normal to their senses, places your processing in the realm beyond reason. It is not reasonable to have lights impact you so harshly. It is beyond reason for you to hear so intensely.

Therefore, you experience what others do not. You experience beyond normal. It is through these sensitivities that you cross the bridge to the realm of intuition. The sensitivities become your intuition.

As you see more, you are able to see what is "not" there. As you hear more, you are able to hear what is "not" there.

As is the case with all your sensitivities. They are hinting at your intuitive consciousness. The more sensitive you become, the more intuitive you become. Thus, by default, the more intuitive you are, the more sensitive you are. Intuition is just being open and receptive to ALL that is out there, not just what is within conscious reasoning.

There is magic in your sensitivities. Another gift from the stars, to be able to remain connected to the beyond, connected to what others may never be able to understand or experience.

It is through honoring these sensitivities that I have fully embraced my intuition and am able to have daily communion with my Spirit Guides. I have conversations with them the same way I might talk to you. I hear them just as I might hear you. It is through honoring these sensitivities that I can channel the loved ones of clients who have crossed over. I can receive visions of the future and I can play in the Akashic Records all day.

The information may come in multiple forms. My main pathway of receptivity is sound. I hear the communication as the spoken word, just as if you and I were having a conversation. My secondary pathway is sight. When I don't have the words to articulate, the information will come to me in images. Images may come in as a metaphor or in the literal.

Another pathway of communication is through knowing. I call them downloads- when the information just shows up as though it's something you've known all along, like a file you can retrieve from your brain.

As an Empath, your primary pathway may be feeling. Information will come through as sensation in the physical form that leads to emotional, mental or spiritual information.

It is rare for me that information comes through my sense of smell. I've found that this is most common when speaking with client's loved ones who have crossed over. They may use a smell as their primary method of communication. Sickness will also come through as a smell. This is the least enjoyable! Sickness does not smell good! It can be putrid and nauseating.

As you open, know that the communication may come to you through any of these channels or pathways. And it might not be just one pathway. Know you are designed to receive this information, to be in communication.

ENERGETIC BOUNDARIES

When it comes to energy, you are in charge. You get to determine the ground rules of communication. Do you want all information to come through? Do you only want information that you can act on to come through? You also get to determine where the information is coming from. Before you begin working any intuitive process, it's important to lay the groundwork, or the ground rules, so to speak.

First, we want to determine who and/or what is answering your questions and what energies you are opening to when you open space for this intuitive process.

Regardless if you are speaking to an emotion, a sensation, or general experience, we want the information first to be relayed through your Higher Self and then to you. This ensures that the messages are in alignment with your highest path and purpose and the highest good of all and not clouded in confusion.

This is not a process where we invite loved ones who have passed over to come in and give advice on what our headache is really about and what the next step is. We are creating a very clear container, with very clear energetic boundaries. It is in learning these boundaries that you not only reach a place of management with your empathic abilities, but you become in charge and decide when you experience it. By practicing these boundaries from the beginning, you send a very clear message to the energy around you that you aren't messing around and you won't put up with anything less than the expectations you have set forth.

For this process, I recommend you set the following rules by stating out loud: *"I request that all messages only come in from my Spirit Guides and my Higher Self, in alignment with divine truth, acting in the Highest Good of All."*

Know that your Spirit Guides are here in service of you. They have been with you your entire life. They have lived here on Earth, just like you, and managed to clear their karma and graduate from this realm and stay in the next. Their mission is to help you serve your mission. They have no other agenda than this. As you feel for their presence, you may tune into how they show up for you, see if you can feel them individually. You may get a sense for their personalities.

They show up how you best receive them and present themselves in a way in which you most need them to show up. They may show up in a human expression, as angels, lights, giants, animals, crystals or simply a feeling. They will communicate with you in the way that you most need in each moment, which may result in shapeshifting. As you grow and transform, they grow and transform to reflect you.

CREATING RITUAL

When you are ready to start communicating, I recommend using ritual. Ritual consists of taking the same three steps every time. This helps to condition the energy and let it know what you are preparing to do. This also makes it easier and easier to connect every time. It will get to the point where you don't even have to finish asking your question before the answer comes in. I am often cut off by my Spirit Guides. I only get out a word or two of my question and the answer is already waiting for me.

The three steps I recommend taking are:
1. Open space
2. Use inquiry
3 .Give gratitude

Opening space is about putting yourself in a receptive state and becoming present and grounded in the process. This ensures the highest level of clarity for the communication you receive. I close my eyes, take three deep belly breaths with slow, gentle exhales then call in my spirit guides.

"I ask that my Guides surround me, encircle me and infuse me with their divine light and divine love. Help me to stay open and receptive to how this communication is showing up for me. Help me to transmute any dissonance or discordant energy as we process the communication. Thank you, thank you, thank you."

I say something a little different every time, just based upon what I am needing in the moment. As I call them in, I feel for their presence. I visualize them encircling me and I lean in to the love and light that I am requesting from them.

Once you get cozied up with your Spirit Guides, you can start asking questions. I often start off my communication with "Show me how" or "Tell me how" then complete it with whatever it is I'm looking for.

"Show me how this is for me."

Then open. Allow the energy to communicate with you. The information will come in a way that you can most easily receive it. It may also come in a way that requires a bit of creativity. Remember that this is a conversation. You may always ask for clarity. You may ask for clarification or confirmation that you understand what is being communicated.

Then end with gratitude: *"Thank you, thank you, thank you."*

Remember that it will take time, intention and lots of practice.

LOVING THE QUESTIONS

"I beg you to have patience with everything unresolved in your heart and try to love the questions themselves as if they were locked rooms or books written in a very foreign language. Don't search for the answers which could not be given to you now, because you would not be able to live them. And the point is to live everything. Live the questions now. Perhaps then, someday far in the future, you will gradually, without even noticing, live your way into the answer."

– Rainier Maria Rilke

Don't expect to have clear answers right away. It's a process, a practice, and there may be times we aren't ready to hear the answers. Simply being in the inquiry opens us up to the healing. It is the first step of allowing the communication that wants to come through to be seen. It's letting it know, *"Hey, I'm here. What you have to say matters."*

This is a place to practice asking quality questions. Being with the process of finding the best questions to ask is almost as valuable, if not more so, than receiving the answers themselves. The quality of your questions determines the quality of your answers and the quality of your life.

If you find yourself asking yes and no and black and white questions, this is a good indicator that the questions you are asking will not yield high quality answers.

High Quality Questions
- Tell me how is this showing up for me.
- Show me what is here for me.
- What does this emotion/energy/experience have to tell me? What does it need from me to feel seen, heard, and loved?
- What does it look like to shift or heal this state?
- What does it look like to allow myself to feel how I want to feel?
- What does it look like to give myself per mission to move through what's coming up?
- Where am I needing to give myself permission?
- What does it look like to be supported through this process?

- What here wants to be seen, witnessed, and honored?
- Am I owning my power or giving it away? How?
- What does it look like to take back my power and my worth?
- How can I take ownership of my piece in this co-creation without taking over-responsibility?
- What boundary is asking to be defined?
- How am I honoring my boundaries? How am I not?
- How can I set myself up for success moving forward?
- What if I don't have to have all the answers? Then what? What does it look like to allow my self to be in the mystery of the unknown?

CLOSING SPACE

When you are complete, end with sincere gratitude.

"Thank you, thank you, thank you. Thank you for showing up for me. Thank you for communicating

with me. Thank you for being a part of bringing me back to myself and back to my highest. Thank you, thank you, thank you."

Say what feels good and always acknowledge how this whole process and all the energies present are conspiring FOR you.

Intuitive Inquiry Process

Set boundaries: *"I request that all messages only come in from my Spirit Guides and my Higher Self, in alignment with divine truth, acting in the Highest Good of All."*

Open space: Take 3 deep belly breaths and state:

"I ask that my Guides surround me, encircle me and infuse me with their divine light and divine love. Help me to stay open and receptive to how this communication is showing up for me. Help me to transmute any dissonance or discordant energy as we process the communication. Thank you, thank you, thank you."

Visualize your Guides. Lean into their love.

Use inquiry: *"Show me how this is for me." "What does the anger have to tell me?"*

Stay open. Remember communication comes in many forms.

End with gratitude: *"Thank you, thank you, thank you. Thank you for showing up for me. Thank you for communicating with me. Thank you for being a part of bringing me back to myself and back to my highest. Thank you, thank you, thank you."*

6
Finding The Beauty In Trauma

"The deepr that sorrow carves into your being, the more joy you can contain."
- Kahlil Gibran

Step Four is seeing trauma in a different light. A light that brings forth tools on your journey of embodying your purpose as a healer.

Are there moments when you reflect on your life and think, *"Good Lord. I've been through hell and back!"* Does it seem like you've been through shit storm after shit storm? At times do you feel plagued by trauma? I do!

Trauma is a deeply distressing or disturbing incident. No one can define if something is traumatic for you, except for you. Do you remember being in grade school and how drama with friends felt like the end of the world? *"My life is over!"* is a phrase that gets thrown around often with pre-teens.

I had a client a couple years ago named Lily. She was subconsciously deeply hurt by something that happened in 7th grade. She had fallen for a boy and her best friend liked the same boy. She liked him first and called dibs, but the boy didn't like her back. He ended up going out with her best friend and she felt completely betrayed. As a result, she took on a belief that she couldn't trust people. This response had her moving through life anticipating betrayal at every turn. It was impacting her ability to fully receive her marriage.

When I found this in her Akashic Records and shared this with her, she was shocked. It all rang completely true, what happened then and how it was impacting her now, but she didn't understand how something so small and minor could have such a grave impact.

It's easy to look back and belittle our past experiences, especially what we went through as children. But as the child, it's your whole world. At that age, you are learning the importance of going off on your own, finding tribe outside of family. This happened at a vital stage in her development where she learned that it wasn't safe to be in community outside of her family, thus creating feelings of isolation.

> *"There is a crack in everything,
> that's how the light gets in."*
> - Leonard Cohen

In studies done at the Foundation for Highly Sensitive Persons, it was determined that Highly Sensitive People are more deeply impacted and adversely affected by trauma. Which means that as an Empath, that applies to you too.

If there had been someone to hold space for Lily at that time, most likely it wouldn't have had the same impact. An emotional haven would have provided her with the ability to process her emotions rather than suppress them, which resulted in the limiting belief. Unfortunately, her mother belittled her experience, not fully grasping onto the full measure of this developmental stage.

It's quite common, when we experience trauma, that those around us are incapable of holding space for us. I call this collateral trauma. Lily's mother thought that if she minimized the experience for Lily, that it would go away. *"Oh, it's no big deal. You'll be friends again soon."* The driving force behind Lily's mother's response was that she simply didn't know how to hold space for Lily. Acknowledging that Lily really needed to be held through this would have pinpointed her inability to give Lily what she needs. This would have triggered her own wounding from childhood that she needed to be perfect, and it becomes a vicious cycle. For Lily, as she was branching out into the world to find her own tribe, she felt betrayed. Then when retreating into the safety of her original tribe, her family, comfort wasn't found as her mother did not know how to hold space for her, alienating her from both worlds.

Collateral trauma is much easier to see as the severity of trauma increases. Often, our own experience of trauma is also traumatic for those around us. When my brother died by suicide, it impacted everyone in the family, close friends, even acquaintances. Guilt, pain, and shame spread like wildfire. Because this trauma also impacted everyone around me, there wasn't anyone to hold space for my trauma as they were dealing with their own. The isolation created additional trauma as there was no one to lean in to; we all fell apart.

Understanding collateral trauma helps us to remove some of the density that is being held around the trauma. It may help you see your own trauma in a new way and give you the opportunity to arrive at a state of compassion. Understanding collateral trauma will help to reduce blame and allow for something else to come into its place, possibly forgiveness.

As Lily could fully honor how the event had impacted her, healing began to take place. She understood the strain in her relationship with her mother. She better understood her resistance to fully connecting with her husband and allowing for vulnerability. As the pieces came together, compassion sprang forth. As her relationships softened, she began to see the beauty that was cultivated from her experiences. It shifted how she showed up as a mother to her daughter. Through her own challenges, she cultivated greater presence as a parent and greater compassion in general.

UNEARTHING SUPPRESSED TRAUMA

How do we know there is trauma if you don't remember it? Or if the trauma is from past lives? Hidden traumas create barriers in the present day.

A few signs that you may have suppressed trauma that is ready to be seen:
- You don't remember a lot of your childhood. This is often a result of spending a lot of time outside of your body due to trauma that oc curred while in your body.
- You have memories of astral projecting- being outside of your body, looking down at your body and the general surroundings
- You've had flashbacks of bits and pieces

without total comprehension of what you flashed back to. Or full on flashbacks.
- You lean towards controlling behavior. You like to have everything planned out and organized and stress out or trigger easily when it's not clean and organized or when things don't go as planned.
- Strange dreams that feel like memories, a hint at past lives.
- You don't want to "stir the pot," "shake shit up," "cause a scene," or "put anyone out," and go out of your way to avoid conflict for fear of potential backlash.
- You experience PTSD without a known source.
- Lifelong, chronic depression.
- Invisible barriers in your life that you continually hit up against but don't know why. A sense of something feeling much harder than what is logical.

These are common reactions to trauma. If you don't remember any childhood trauma, these scenarios could be showing you there is more beneath the surface calling to be seen.

TRANSMUTING TRAUMA

"It is in the middle of misery that so much becomes clear. The one who says nothing good came of this, is not yet listening."
-Clarissa Pinkola Estes

As you take a moment to look back at how trauma has influenced your life, it's time to start asking, *"How has this served me? How has this brought me back to myself?"*

When reflecting on past trauma, it's easy to see the adverse effects. Common responses are shutting down, disconnecting, and losing a luster for life. What can be tricky to see is the alchemical process that is also taking place; how the chunk of coal is becoming a diamond through the intense pressure placed upon it. This is where we find the beauty.

After my brother died by suicide, I sat in guilt and blame. I blamed myself for his death because

Journaling

What connections to your own history are being made? Are there indications that you have suppressed trauma from this lifetime? Do you sense that you may have suppressed trauma from past-lives? Are you already aware of specific events that are calling to you to be seen and healed?

I knew he was suicidal and I didn't know how to stop him. The guilt, and sometimes the envy of how he left, rotted my core. I punished myself by pulling my life apart. I married an alcoholic who could punish me with lies, deceit and abuse. I punished myself by sabotaging my job. I went from climbing the corporate ladder to digging a hole for it to fall into. I did this for six years, until I ended up almost jobless and homeless.

Sometimes I ask, *"Why? Why was I so determined to pull my life apart?"* But, the even better question is, *"How did pulling my life apart serve me? How was it the best thing that ever happened to me?"*

Looking back now, it's so easy to see that I pulled my life apart so I could put it back together from a new perspective and a more healed state. I put it together free from so much of the conditioning about who I was supposed to be and how I should be living my life. I put it back together free from the weight of the trauma.

It was in this time, of life falling apart, that I learned to heal my PTSD. I had a blank canvas in which to create my world and took the time to figure out what I really wanted in life. It was during this time that I started dating my current husband. I spent hours scripting what a perfect day would look like. I scripted what it felt like to be in a healthy, loving relationship. I scripted what it felt like to have my own business and be my own boss. One year later, everything from that script was coming true.

I pulled my life apart so I could fill those cracks with gold. Looking back at it all, every trauma was the best thing that ever happened to me. And every day I get to choose if that remains true.

"Only when we are brave enough to explore the darkness will we discover the infinite power of our light."
-Brené Brown

Some days, it doesn't feel true. Some days, stuff comes up from those events and I think, *"Oh shit! I thought I was done with this!"*

And then I breathe. I call in my guides, I glean the lessons and I come back to myself. I come back to seeing it once again as being the best thing that ever happened to me. And from an even higher perspective, with even more fullness than before.

Spiritual Teacher Gabby Bernstein has a fabulous mantra for when she falls out of alignment, *"Great practice."* I've adapted this to *"Great practice, thank you. Great practice, thank you. Great practice, thank you."* This simple mantra makes it so easy to come back to a space where I'm willing to see the joy and choose the joy. I don't choose it every moment of everyday. We're still human after all. But I always come back. And you can too. It's all just practice. Great practice!

BUT, WHAT HAPPENED WASN'T OKAY!

Finding beauty does not mean that what happened was okay. It does not mean it lets anyone off the hook who was involved in the trauma. This is NOT about taking responsibility for something that isn't yours to take responsibility for. It's not even about forgiveness. Finding the beauty is saying, *"This terrible thing happened AND…"*

AND, I used it to help others going through the same thing.

AND, I used it to fuel my passion to make sure this doesn't happen to anyone else.

AND, I used it to learn how to heal.

AND, I used it to anchor more deeply into joy by learning what joy isn't.

AND, I used it to find gratitude in the small things.

AND, I used it to figure out who I am and what I want in this world.

AND, I used it to realize that only I can determine my worth.

AND, I used it to open up even more to those around me whom I really love.

You may not have your AND statement yet. It may not even be the right time for you to complete this alchemical process. And that is 100% okay.

There is a balance between honoring what took place by allowing all the suppressed emotion to come forward, and honoring what took place by completing the alchemical process, shifting into a positive state, and coming back into the light. Both are needed and it's not something we can force or control. This is a process of permission and allowance for everything that wants to be seen. There may be some yelling, kicking, screaming, and sobbing that gets to take place before you find your AND.

It may be time for you to rage. Rage to honor the crossing or breaking down of your boundaries. Rage against the unfairness, the hurt, the pain, the grief, the sorrow. Rage until your throat is raw and body weak. Then rage again, this time, against the dying of your light. It is here that we find the AND.

*"Do not go gentle into that good night.
Rage, rage against the dying of the light."*
-Dylan Thomas

MESSAGES FROM BEYOND

In a strange way, I've been lucky. The contributors to my biggest traumas are crossed over. Through their death, it has been easier for me to receive healing and allow the fullness of the truth to come to light. It has also been easier for me to connect to their Higher Selves. As needed, I can call them into my space for continued healing work. They have both assisted in the continual unraveling of my trauma.

Last year, one contributor, my ex-husband Tyler, decided to pay me a visit. I met Tyler after losing my big brother to suicide. Tyler had lost his little sister to suicide and we came together in our misery. After losing ourselves from the loss of our siblings, we thought we could find ourselves in each other.

Our relationship was full of laughter, deep conversations, art, music, adventure, and love. It was also full of depression, drama, lying, stealing, suicidal ideations, alcoholism, rehab after rehab after rehab, and one large dose of abuse. I stayed for two years. After the divorce, he only stayed on Earth for two more years. He took his life as well.

After he crossed over, he would drop by from time to time. It was most often unannounced. At times unwelcome. Often, our visits would start with a mixed bag of anger, frustration, grief, sadness and rage.

When he came to visit me in my Mexican apartment, it started just the same. Immediately upon his arrival, like clockwork, I burst into tears.

"What do you want? What do you have to say?"

He claimed that I was ready to hear the deeper truths about our marriage and how these deeper truths were necessary to my life's purpose.

I wanted to push him away even more. How dare he show up here, unannounced, with his "great wisdom" to bestow upon me! How dare he use these deeper truths as justification for all the lies, for the alcoholism, for "that night" of which we rarely speak, leaving me with years of PTSD.

This is where he joined me in tears. We sat across from each other and cried. He looked straight at me. I tried not to look at him. It still hurts my heart to look at him. It still hurts his heart to remember "that night."

"It was all part of the bigger plan, Alise. I came as a servant to your mission. I told you a year ago, my life purpose was our divorce. But there's more. It has to do with you and why you're still here."

"All the lies that I told you, day after day after day.... those lies were for you to question everything. By questioning everything, you began to anchor into your intuition. You began to choose your truth above all else. You began to discern

the illusion of this world from universal wisdom. It's because of those lies that you'll no longer accept the bullshit, from anyone, anywhere."

"The alcoholism was how I dealt with what I was here to do. It wasn't easy to be the bad guy, the perpetrator, the antagonist in your story. I had to lower my vibration to be capable of bringing you the contrast. It wasn't pre-determined, how it would all happen. All we knew before we came was that my role was to help you break out of your own darkness."

"As for that night..." He looked down at his hands and sighed.

"Without me having wrapped my hands around your throat, you wouldn't have known how desperately you wanted to live. Life was so dark for you. We were both so stuck in our misery, in the grief and the loss. It was the fastest way. You got your fight back in you that night. You needed your fight back."

"You need to know that I did it all for you. Until you see this piece you can't lock all your understanding into place."

"There are those that come to Earth as the warriors, and there are those that come to support the warriors. Both roles are of equal importance as one cannot exist without the other. You are the warrior and you are here to begin to pave the path for a utopian society. For this to happen, there must be a rejection of all the dystopic ways you are participating in. Without me, you could not have seen your own participation in the illusion. I was the servant to your mission. Everything, all of it, it happened for you."

"I'm here because my purpose isn't complete, until yours is too."

This conversation was a turning point for me. I am continually shown how this trauma has served me. The more I heal, the more beauty I find. From this interaction I gained a new perspective on trauma, how it's been the catalyst for my work as a Healer and how it's been necessary to fully understand life on Earth.

As I brought my natural healing gifts from my home planet, I quickly learned they cannot be directly applied to this Earthly Realm. On Earth we are all so different. What worked for me "back home" isn't the same here.

Trauma on Earth has shown me how soul wounding takes place and what can be done to bring healing. Trauma has fueled my fire and drive to study healing modalities of all kinds and find what bridges my world and this one.

My ex-husband was the servant to my healing mission. His purpose was not to be a Healer, but to help the Healers learn to heal. He only serves his mission well when I receive the beauty of that gift. I see so easily now, how trauma can be the catalyst that helps healers activate their gifts and find their path for healing, so they can help others heal too.

TRAUMA ACTIVATES OUR GIFTS

Have you heard stories of people dying and coming back to life? When they return it's as though the veil has been lifted and they are more sensitive to the other side. They may come back with the ability to communicate with dead people or see things in a whole new way.

In an article written by Psychic Medium, James Van Praagh, he states that: *"There are many accounts of people having near-death experiences and returning with facts they did not know before. People even come back with clairvoyant gifts – knowledge of future events, even an understanding of quantum physics. Research has shown that NDE survivors have three times the number of psychic experiences as the general population. Clearly, their perspective from the other side had given them some insights that they carried back with them – just like my own awareness of how my thoughts and deeds all became part of my "life tapestry."*

Intense trauma acts in a similar way. When we experience intense trauma, it can "knock us out" of our bodies, giving entrance to the other side. This is called an Out-of-Body Experience. It helps to activate the intuitive and healing gifts you came to Earth with.

My oldest memory is from an Out-of-Body Experience, when I was sexually abused as a four-year-old. I remember shooting out of my body, high above the ceiling, as though the ceiling didn't exist. I looked down and could see the top of the head of the man holding me and my small body in his arms. I could see the hallway on the other side of the room and the rooms beyond. I've had three other vivid Out-of-Body Experiences since then and only as a child.

Most of my memories after that are fragments. Bits and pieces here and there. Most of which consisted of me being alone and in communion with the other side.

I believe that being thrown out of my body from such intense trauma is what gave me access to my gifts. The trauma acted as a tool to activate my abilities early on. It also acted as a tool to isolate me. To ensure I didn't feel safe, so that I retreated into the safety of the ethers and other realms. Retreating to the ethers and other realms honed my intuition. My isolation as a child helped me manage my sensitivities, again so I could hone my intuition even further.

This may not be true for everyone. It is what I have found to be true for me. These are the gifts I have found for myself in trauma. These are the ways I see that I have been served by childhood sexual abuse. Not only did this abuse serve as the foundation for me anchoring into my gifts, it created the opportunity for me to learn how to heal from it.

Trauma after trauma gave me the opportunities to learn how to heal. To know it's possible to get on the other side of it all. No matter the intensity. It brought me to the tools that helped me to heal shadows deeper than my own. I didn't need to experience the most severe of traumas to be given the tools to help heal all traumas. I just needed the trauma to lead me to the tools.

CREATING A BETTER OUTCOME

No matter how broken you feel, know that we all go through things that break us. It's up to us to decide if it breaks us down or breaks us open. Even after something has broken you down, you can still have it break you open. We are broken open when we see how the experience has made us more beautiful than before. By seeing how breaking has given us everything we need to be the healers we came here to be.

In Japan, they call this practice wabi-sabi. Wabi-Sabi means to find beauty in the broken. This philosophy is applied to broken objects. When a bowl or mug is broken, they practice kintsugi, or "golden joinery" which is the method of restoring a broken piece with a lacquer that is mixed with gold, silver or platinum. The gold-filled crack becomes a testament to its history, applying a level of awe, reverence and restoration. What was beautiful before, is now considered even more so. It is a highly revered art form that has been practiced for over 500 years.

When this practice is applied to trauma, the cracks break us open, so our light may shine through even brighter. More beauty can be found.

As we seek out the beauty and gifts from trauma, it's important to ask new questions. When we ask the typical, *"Why did this happen to me?"* or exclaim *"This never should have happened!"*, we get stuck in the density of the past. This leaves us incapable of being present in the moment, here and now, where the trauma is no longer taking place.

Instead, ask yourself:
"How has this served me?"
"How did this show up for me?"
"What has this experience given me?"

When you feel comfortable with the process, you may want to ask, *"How was this the best thing that ever happened to me?"*

When I stopped exclaiming, *"This never should have happened to me!"* I could finally ask:

"How did I allow this to transform me?"

"How did I allow this to catapult me into the direction of my purpose?"

"How did I allow this to be a part of my becoming, a becoming of the fullest version of myself within this physical expression?"

Due to the trauma I experienced, I embraced my intuition. The isolation that followed sexual abuse was all encompassing. I hid in closets and retreated into nature. Any escape I could find away from people, led me deeper into myself and deeper into my connection with the world around me. Visitors from other realms became my norm. Hearing footsteps from residual energies to playing with balls of light, my childhood was full of energetic and spiritual exploration.

Journaling

Take a moment to reflect upon your past challenges and traumas. Bring lots of breath to the process. Use the questions above and be with the inquiry of how you could allow those challenges to transform you today. Don't expect answers right away. You may find emotion that wants to come forward first. Stay with your breath to help facilitate those emotions.

The more trauma I experienced, the more I drew inward, until I finally imploded like a supernova. Blasting away the mask, the shell, the coping mechanisms for my light to finally shine through. The trauma was a breaking down of intuitive blocks so I could break open and shine my light in the world. So, I could finally see clearly. Rather than through the lenses of society, convention and tradition, I began to see through the lenses of my divinity.

The divinity that told me, *"My child you are not from here. But you came here with an epic mission. A mission to help heal the planet. It is through the experiential understanding of the density of this world that you will break open to shine your light so mother fucking bright that you can make a real difference in the world. You have been given gifts. Gifts that will ascertain the fulfillment of your purpose. Those gifts are held within your trauma and within your empathic nature. We will guide you, but you must be willing to listen."*

You see, you too, have gone through both past and present life trauma to aide you in the refinement. To help carve you into the beautiful creature you are today, that has full capability of shifting the planet. The ripple effect you can create is beyond your wildest dreams.

Healing Exercise

The contributors to your traumas do not have to be crossed over to connect with their Higher Selves and allow for deeper unfolding. You may open Sacred Space and invite their Higher Selves into sacred space for the intention of finding the beauty and to allow for continued healing.

There is not a script for this, but there are a few guidelines:
- Allow yourself to say everything you've always wanted to say but haven't given your self permission to say, or simply haven't been given the opportunity to. Get it all out. The good, the bad, the ugly. Let your emotions flow.

- Take regular deep breaths. Come back, again and again, into union with your body.
- Ask high quality questions.
- Be open. Release force and control and allow surrendering.
- Lean on your Guides for support.
- Know information can come through many channels.
- Allow yourself to explore the inquiry.

Answers are not needed for healing to begin.

Only do this if it feels safe. Tune into your inner guidance. Ask yourself, *"Does doing this now serve the Highest Good?"* You may want support through this process and that is perfect. Working with trauma gets to happen in a tight container. If you don't feel safe doing this on your own, find a professional to assist. I'm happy to help you with this.

How to Open + Close Sacred Space

Sacred space is space held with a powerful intention to connect with the Divine using ritual. The intention is to align with divine love, light and truth for the highestlevel of healing for the highest good of all.

1. Close your eyes.
2. Take three deep belly breaths, pausing between your inhale and exhale.
3. State, *"I ask that divine love, ligh,t and truth guide me, for the highest level of healing to be achieved in alignment with the highest the level of good for all."*
4. Open to and engage in communication.
5. When you are finished state, *"I am complete. Thank you, thank you, thank you."*

7
Embracing Your Role as a Healer

"When our eyes see our hands doing the work of our hearts, the circle of creation is completed inside us. The doors of our soul fly open, and love steps forth to heal everything in sight."
-Siddhartha Gautamo

"There is no greater gift you can give or receive than to honor your calling. It's why you were born. And how you become most truly alive."
-Oprah

Step Five is about stepping into your role as a Healer. I know. Deep breath. So many questions come up when considering yourself a Healer and how to step into that role. Before you pull back, stay with me just a moment.

What if being a Healer has nothing to do with fixing anything?

What if helping others heal means that you are simply showing up as who you really are, in the most authentic, soulful capacity of yourself?

What if being a Healer means you can start right now?

What if healing is an automatic unraveling that happens to take place under the right conditions?

THE SPIRAL DYNAMIC OF HEALING
"We do not grow absolutely, chronologically. We grow sometimes in one dimensions, and not in another; unevenly. We grow partially. We are relative. We are mature in one realm, childish in another. The past, present, and future mingle, and pull us backward, forward, or fix us in the present. We are made up of layers, cells, constellations."
-Anais Nin

Healing is not a logical, succinct, clean, linear process, with a cookie-cutter step-by-step guide that can be followed by anyone and everyone. It is something that happens, organically, in layers, through the unraveling of many different facets. We do not fully heal from one trauma to then move on to the next trauma, with a starting and an end. It moves in an upward spiral. We heal a little at a time, moving through whatever we are prepared to move through, based on our current skillsets. Ultimately, we will come back to each trauma again and again as we gain more and more skill to work through every aspect. Trauma is multi-faceted and has a lot to share.

Are you familiar with the story of the blind men and the elephant? It is the story of a group of blind men, who have never come across an elephant before. They learn what the elephant is like by touching it. Each blind man feels a different part of the elephant's body, but only one part, such as an ear, the trunk, the tail, or the tusk. They then describe the elephant to each other based on their partial experience, resulting in complete disagreement.

They argue and argue about their experiences, yet they are all experiencing and holding an elephant, just different aspects of it. Healing is just like this. You can only deal with and see so much elephant at one time. You may argue with yourself that you have healed, but it can be quite difficult to see the entire elephant. You learn to heal piece by piece, moving from one part of the elephant and on to the next, until you know the whole elephant.

This movement takes place in an upward spiraling process. As you work your way through healing, you are taken to a new angle, circling around and upward. At this new height and new angle, you are given a different perspective, a higher perspective. You can see it from a new angle, therefore you are able to learn and glean more wisdom from the experience.

By spiraling upward, you can see all sides of the elephant, from all angles to gain the full perspective.

When something comes back up again, don't kick yourself for not having figured it out the first time. This is a GREAT sign. It shows that you have gained more wisdom and learned more tools to work through another aspect of trauma. You have grown and are ready to pull more wisdom and receive more of your gifts. Every time it shows up, there is more for you to gain.

THE HEALER ARCHETYPES

You don't have to work through all your stuff before helping someone else work through theirs. Truly.

Your gift is such an integral part of you that it's hard to recognize it as a gift. It comes naturally and feels so innate that you probably don't realize that it is in fact a gift and doesn't come naturally to everyone else.

This natural way of being, your specific healing gift, can be found within one of eight Healer Archetypes. These archetypes are the energies that came from Divine Source upon our individuation, as we became our own souls. Your dominant archetype is what you expressed and explored on your home planet.

Every Healer has an aspect of all eight within them. However, there is a dominant archetype, that when activated and utilized, your soul has the greatest self-expression, allowing massive amounts of flow and joy in your life. There are light sides and shadow sides to each archetype. Often when we are in a state of depression we are acting in our shadow; thus, we do not recognize the light side of our gifts.

Your Healer Archetype can be found in the Akashic Records as part of your Soul Blueprint. For now, be open to all the possibilities. We aren't looking for specific answers in this moment, simply resonance; a confirmation of soul truth.

These archetypes are ways in which you can work with light. It's not about something that you do, it's about who you are. By showing up as your most authentic self, you are by default a facilitator of light.

As you step into the role of holding space for others and allowing your archetype to come forward, intuition guides the process for you. You don't have to "know" anything. The wisdom is all around you, you simply open to being who you are as you are naturally designed to receive it.

ONE: You are driven by having a mission of service: service to the environment, animals and/or mankind. You are deeply connected to Mother Earth. You are her fierce protector and greatest ally. A spiritual warrior. Your wisdom shares that it is only by caring for Mother Earth that we can really care for one another. The energies you embody are the same energies of Mother Earth, compassion, unconditionality, and tolerance. As Mother Earth is here to provide all living creatures all that they need to survive (food, shelter, community), you are also concerned about ensuring the same for others.

You are deeply connected to the physicality of spirituality. Being in a physical body is a spiritual experience for you. Your spiritual connection comes from your connection to the natural physical world, from the core of the Earth to the stars in the sky. You find Source in what you can see, touch, hear, smell and taste; in what you can physically experience.

As a Healer, you help people connect to their tribe, their roots and an understanding of oneness at the physical level.

You may find yourself drawn to working with childbirth, childcare, nursing, hospice, social work, farming, environmental work, and advocacy work.

TWO: You are driven by creation. You love birthing new creation and new experiences in the physical world. You love exploring and indulging in all that life offers. Movement is very important to you: it is what allows vital life force energy to continue to course through you. You connect to Source and spirituality through physical pleasure: money, sex, and good health. You teach others the joy of being human and how to have a loving connection to the human body.

As a Healer, you connect to all the places within others that are blocking their current experience of joy and may use physicality to bring them back to themselves and to Source.

You may find yourself drawn to helping others embrace their physicality through athletics, yoga, dance, tantra, money manifestation, or even adventure travel.

THREE: You are driven by bringing balance and beauty to the world around you. You have a deep understanding of how choice affects the balance and beauty of the greater whole, making you an expert at understanding the energy of karma. You have a fondness of peace, order and law that helps to maintain this higher balance.

As a Healer, you see in others what is preventing balance and harmony within themselves and how that lack of balance extends to all relationships. You see balance and harmony as the seeds that must be planted to grow into one's full potential.

You may find yourself drawn to the visual arts, law and order, or anything to do with planning and organization.

FOUR: You are driven by interdependent relationship. You see everything as being in relationship with everything else and strive to bring nurturing and love to all. You love to love, nurture, and give of yourself to others.

As a Healer, you are a natural space holder, where you hold a sacred space for others in which they can reclaim the pieces of themselves that they have made wrong or that they have disowned. You feel the places within others they reject. The spaces where they have labeled themselves as bad; the aspects that have been disowned. You see where others are blocked to giving and receiving love towards themselves as well as others. By holding this loving space, you bring others back into their wholeness through loving self-acceptance and non-judgment. This is your healing gift: helping others recognize that they are whole, they are not broken and never have been, and there is nothing to fix.

You may find yourself drawn to service work, therapy, counseling, coaching and parenting.

FIVE: You are driven by communication, self-expression, and teaching. You have a very special relationship with language - words will have taste and substance for you. You love to express yourself creatively and you love to offer advice and guidance.

As a Healer, you are a natural channel and have a gift with taking the energetic, ethereal, and abstract and putting it into a language that others can receive. Through this gift with words, you naturally inspire and move people into action, especially by helping them shift at the level of the mind, opening them to new perspectives and allowing for miracles.

You may find yourself drawn to speaking, writing, teaching, counseling, and channeling.

SIX: You are driven by bringing the truth to light. Societal norms and niceties aren't often taken into consideration on this path to truth. You see each person as having their own individual truth and want to help them take a stand for that truth. You don't fall for others bullshit and can easily identify when people are bullshitting themselves.

As a Healer you help others identify the places within themselves that do not align with their truth, rejecting the beliefs thrusted upon them by family and society. You hold others in their authenticity. You also have a natural ability to "see." You see beyond the everyday and may be gifted with clairvoyance.

You may find yourself drawn to activism, quality assurance, speaking, and fortune telling.

SEVEN: You are driven by freedom. You love to consciously manifest money to pave the path to freedom. You have an innate connection and high sensitivity to energy and can quickly shift your physical state to create an intended reaction.

You are all about quick, new action for big, new results and living life on your terms.

As a Healer, you use your sensitivities to tune into the energy of others and what shifts they can make to create the results that they want. Through this energy shifting, you show others how to become the powerful creators of reality that they are. You also show them the power of utilizing intuition in the manifestation process.
You may find yourself drawn to entrepreneurism and anything that allows to you work outside the box.

EIGHT: You are driven by logic and give insightful, succinct advice, rooted in the principles of Universal Law. You have a natural understanding of the Laws of the Universe and see the dissonance between this higher wisdom and the way that society operates.

As a Healer, you hold space for others to find their inner guidance and learn to create their own experience. By asking great questions and inserting profound wisdom, you help others break free from illusions, false perceptions and negative beliefs.

You may find yourself drawn to coaching, mentoring, mediation, and meditation.

EMBODYING YOUR HEALER ARCHETYPE

The best way to step into your role as a Healer is to learn a healing modality, specifically a modality that includes an attunement.

A healing modality is simply a method through which healing can be experienced or expressed. There are dozens, if not hundreds, of healing modalities. I recommend choosing a healing modality that requires and comes with an attunement.

An attunement is an energetic initiation into the modality. This is incredibly important for Empaths who are experiencing depression. The attunement acts like a key that unlocks the door to higher vibrations. It gives you immediate access to the additional vital life force energy that is needed to help you out of the depression. The attunement will help to release some of the density around your trauma, so your healing can naturally begin.

The modality gives you the structure, the attunement gives you the key to fully access the structure now, without having to have it all figured out yet. Having both creates a doorway out of overwhelm and depression so you can step into your purpose now and forge a path to finally get on the other side of feeling broken.

My favorite modality to use is the Akashic Records. The Records are a wonderful for both the beginner and the expert.

The Akashic Records are infinite and hold the soul truth about everything in existence. There is structure that can help navigate the depth of information that is available to us, while also leaving lots of room for exploration.

With the Records, you have the opportunity to:
- Learn how your soul best expresses itself in the Earthly realm.
- See where you are from and identify your Healer Archetypes.
- Discover the past and present-life events that are creating barriers in your present day.
- Receive guidance for how to best move toward your desires.
- Clear the trauma in your soul's DNA, while leaving the learning intact.
- Discover and understand your soul contracts and karmic backpack.

When we have suppressed our traumas, our histories, and our emotions, the Akashic Records are an incredibly useful tool for unearthing what took place.

The Akashic Records are self-regulated. They will only show you what your soul is currently capable of handling and what the Practitioner can hold space for. For example, if you have a severe trauma that revisiting would act like Pandora's

Box, your Records will present with a past-life experience dealing with very similar energies. This is a soft way for you to begin to unravel the traumas and wounding in a safe, slow and steady way that doesn't undo your life.

In addition, with past lives, there typically isn't a memory, so there isn't an emotional charge. It can be processed at the intellectual level, which creates space, allowing for suppressed emotions to process. As you feel safe in this healing, feeling safe working with the bigger trauma is possible.

HELPING OTHERS HEAL HELPS HEAL YOU

Whichever modality you choose, the more you apply what you learn, the deeper you will integrate the learning. Doing healing work helps move the concepts into the experiential. It shows us where we have gaps in our understanding, allowing us to dive deeper into the modality. As you apply these healing processes, your own healing will naturally unfold.

Those you serve are incredible mirrors for your healing process. You will magnetize people who are going through very similar situations to you or are learning the same lessons you are learning.

My favorite question to ask myself after every session I have with a client is, "*How was this session FOR ME?*" There is always so much wisdom available that applies to me as well. Often, sessions with clients helps me to see something in myself that I hadn't seen before. I can also ask how what my clients were dealing with applies to me.

So much wisdom can be gleaned for your own healing process when showing up in service of others. This process only enhances the way you can show up for people. Not only are you actively showing up for yourself, the more you receive in the energetic exchange of serving others, the more energy you have available to continue to serve, and the greater your willingness to show up and hold sacred space and receive messages for them. This is another upward spiraling dynamic.

GET OUT OF YOUR OWN WAY

"Notice it. Look straight at it. Breathe into it, and it will change. It will change."
– Victoria Erickson

You have spent a good chunk of your life sitting in a haze of confusion and depression. You now understand how to move forward, it's simply time to do it. In the process of putting these five steps into action, there will be obstacles along the way. Knowing what to anticipate will help you set yourself up for success.

OBSTACLE #1-
LEARNING TO ASK BETTER QUESTIONS

You may be saying to yourself, *"This is all great, but really, who am I? People may think I'm crazy. I feel too broken. I feel too depressed."* It's time to ask better questions.

When you ask, *"Who am I to be a healer?"* the weight of the world comes crashing down on your shoulders. The answer can only be as good as the question. So instead we ask, *"Who am I not to do what I came here to do? What gives me the right to refuse my calling and my gifts?"* You're not alone in thinking and feeling this way.

OBSTACLE #2-
CATCHING UP WITH YOUR OWN GROWTH

Every single intuitive Empath I have worked with has a past lifetime of persecution for using their gifts. Many have been hunted, hung, buried alive, cast out of society, disowned by their families, locked away, or tortured.

So much of your mindset is anchored in this past-life trauma. Anchored in the assumption that what was true back then, 100 years, 500 years, 1,000 years ago is still true today. It is time for you to catch up with yourself. Catch up with where you are today, who you are today. See the proof in the world around you that it's safe to share your gifts and shine your light.

Spirituality has become the new hip. The more you own your woo, the more you are lifted up.

It's time to find your people. I am your people. And this new awareness of where you are today will help to break down old coping mechanisms and programming from the lifetimes before.

OBSTACLE # 3-
APPLYING WHAT YOU LEARNED

Where will you set aside time in your schedule? Right now, pull out your calendar. Where will you create space for managing your sensitivities? What are your plans for moving forward to integrate the five steps from this book?

OBSTACLE #4-
HOLDING YOURSELF ACCOUNTABLE

How will you keep yourself accountable to applying these steps, specifically the ethereal steps of processing the healing that wants to take place?

By pursuing a modality, like the Akashic Records, you can have the accountability and community of those that are in your class.

OBSTACLE #5-
FINDING YOUR TRIBE, GETTING SUPPORT

You are not alone in this. You were not meant to be alone in this. All the times you spent alone, feeling isolated and broken, helped you to become who you are and will continue to serve you as you move ever upward on the spiral of healing. There is no need to continue the isolation or brokenness. It's time for us to come together, unite, form our own tribe of healers, movers and shakers, and own our dharma.

Having help will ensure you set aside the time to be with your gifts. It will hold you accountable to allowing the messages from the world around you, to move you inward and heal the world within you. Having help reminds you are not alone.

You can do it on your own. But do you want to? Join me at: www.thecosmicwomb.com.

Journaling

What obstacles do you foresee affecting you the most? What can you put in place to set yourself up for success?

Conclusion

"This year, carry your aliveness around like flowers, bursting from open ribs. And scatter those seeds across so many miles and roads that others pick them up along the way, so they too can remember how to bloom, as though our wild Earth depended upon it. Because it does."
-Victoria Erickson

You were born from the stars to help heal this world. You've brought wonderful gifts with you. You are here to be yourself, 100%. And in being yourself, your light shines so bright, it helps to heal the world. Your history of trauma, your history of being overwhelmed by your gifts, gets to be just that, your history.

Being an Empath is the most powerful gift you have. As you manage your sensitivities, you can use your empathic channel as a tool for accelerated healing. Both for yourself and for the world. Your depression has served as a message from your soul to look back and find the treasure in your traumas. Let those traumas be where you've broken open and let the light shine through. That gorgeous golden light. You now see how the trauma itself can be a tool for helping to forge you into the healer you are here to be.

You now have clear steps and a path to move forward:
1. Get in union with your body.
2. Manage your sensitivities.
3. Use being empathic as a tool for accelerated healing.
4. Find the beauty in trauma.
5. Step into your role as healer.

You know now that your next step is to learn a healing modality. Doing so will continue to lift the depression, hone your healing gifts and help you step into your purpose as a Healer, crafting a life you love.

I'm here to support you in the process and would love to be by your side through all of it. Come find me. Let's do this together. www.thecosmic-womb.com.

"Offer the wisdom you've distilled from your own suffering as nectar and balm to heal the world's wounds.

All of your experiences have led you to this place- you have become the gift your world needs in order to become whole.

You have risen, like good bread, from being kneaded, hard, by life's knuckles. You have breathed through broken ribs and burning lungs to become soul food, to become a source of pure nourishment.

You know, from your own rising, how to alchemize what ails our world- how to transform divisiveness, fear, despair, violence, slavery, suffering into the nectar of love."

– Hiro Boga

Acknowledgements

First, I want to thank you, my reader, my fellow Empath, and my new friend. Thank you for receiving me into your life by reading this book. For as much as I tried to hold you through this journey and fully see you, I know you see me too.

Second, I want to thank my husband Chad, my biggest supporter and my biggest fan. Thank you for being the most supportive man I could ever ask for. Thank you for holding me while I questioned my sanity. Thank you for holding space for this book journey, which took me to another country and required many months apart. I applaud your patience with me and forever hold you in my heart and arms, as I know I am held in yours.

Thank you to each and every one of my clients. Thank you for your trust and vulnerability. For allowing me to hold space for you, which in turn helped me along my own journey and expanded my belief in what is possible.

Thank you to my Book Coaches. Angela Lauria, who I started this book journey with. Thank you for teaching me the genius of the Difference Process. Yes, it works! Danielle Fournier, for holding me as I gave birth to this life-long dream. For helping me find my motivation and ensuring I finished, despite my protests and distractions.

Thank you to my friends. Eleanor Miller, for being the one I can say absolutely anything and everything to and it doesn't sound crazy. For holding me in all of my woo and seeing me through the process. Teba Coulson, for keeping me grounded, helping me constantly process my shit and always being a great friend. Thank you to Kelli Reese and Jiayuh Chyan, my fellow Akashic Record Coaches, who helped me find even more joy and excitement in the Records and for forging the path of sharing the Records and writing about it.

Thank you to all my other friends and family who held me through this, cheered me along and continue to help me embrace my most authentic self. I am so blessed and so grateful.

Thank you, thank you, thank you!

About the Author

Alisabeth Shelman is an Intuitive Healer, Akashic Records Coach and Teacher and a Reiki Master. She is dedicated to helping Empaths transmute their traumas into tools that can help them heal themselves and others. Alisabeth teaches powerful healing modalities, like the Akashic Records, with empathic women like you, to help them embrace their gifts and amplify the light in the world.

She believes we all have a special gift and that it's critical we use our traumas and challenges to fortify our gifts and catapult ourselves into the light, where we are sharing those gifts with the world. Our lives should be dedicated to our gifts. To finding them and sharing them with the world.

It's the only reason we're here. It's what makes life worth living. It's what makes everything else in the world matter.

Alisabeth forged her own path to the other side of broken. Having spent half of her life depressed, struggling with suicidal ideation and feeling cursed by her intuitive abilities and sensitivities, she knows what it takes to move from depression and overwhelm into purpose and joy.

Now there is little she enjoys more than using her gifts and serving her clients. When she isn't playing in the Akashic Records, you can find her traveling the world, spending time with her husband and daughter, eating chocolate, and reading romance novels.

You can find out more about Alisabeth and the work she does with clients at:
www.thecosmicwomb.com.

You may also message her at:
alise@thecomsicwomb.com.

Printed in Great Britain
by Amazon